Producer & International Distributor
eBookPro Publishing
www.ebook-pro.com

Haggadah for Passover – The Am Yisrael Chai Haggadah:
The Concise Israeli Haggadah for a Meaningful Seder Celebrating the Continuity of the Jewish People and Israel's Contribution to the World

Copyright © 2025 MILAH TOVAH PRESS

All rights reserved; No parts of this book may be reproduced or transmitted in any form or by any means, electronic or mechanical, including photocopying, recording, taping, or by any information retrieval system, without the permission, in writing, of the author.

Cover & Illustrations: Maria Sokhatski
Editor: Dani Silas

Contact: agency@ebook-pro.com
ISBN 9789655754889

Introduction

Welcome to "The Israeli Passover Haggadah" – a celebration of tradition, faith, and the enduring spirit of Israel. Each year, as we gather together with family and friends around the Seder table, we reconnect with our rich Jewish heritage and bask in the togetherness of Jewish life. With this Haggadah, take Passover one step further by embracing the rich, vibrant tapestry of Israeli culture.

In this unique Haggadah, we blend timeless tradition with the modern narrative of Israel – the homeland of the Jewish people and a beacon of hope and innovation. Through captivating Israeli success stories and fun facts about the Holy Land, spend this Seder night embracing a deeper connection to your heritage – both ancient and modern.

Throughout the pages, you will encounter all the familiar passages of the Haggadah alongside illuminating insights into Israel's contributions to the world – from technological innovations and cultural significance to humanitarian endeavors and artistic achievements.

The English transliteration will always appear parallel to the original Hebrew text, with the English translation following below.

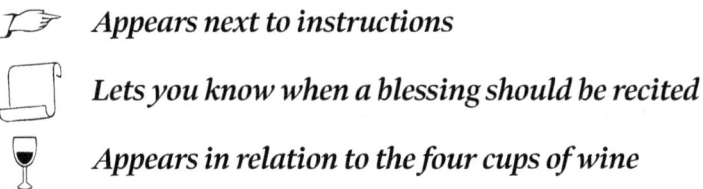

Appears next to instructions

Lets you know when a blessing should be recited

Appears in relation to the four cups of wine

You can find all of your favorite Passover songs (Chad Gadya, Who Knows One?, Go Down Moses, Eliyahu Ha-Navi) all together in the Songs chapter, so you can skip back and forth and incorporate them in your Seder as you go along.

Chag Sameach, and Am Yisrael Chai!

Contents

Kadesh - Blessing on the Wine 6
Urchatz - Washing Hands 12
Israel in Progressiveness 14
Karpas - The Leafy Vegetable 16
Yachatz - Breaking the Middle Matzah 18
Israel in High-Tech 20
Magid - Telling the Story of Exodus 22
Israel in Innovation 28
Israel in Culture 42
Dayeinu 44
Israel in Academia 58
Rachtzah - Washing Hands (this time, with a blessing) 60
Motzi-Matzah - Blessing on the Matzah 62
Israel in Philanthropy 64
Maror - Bitter Herb 66
Korech - Maror Wrapped in Matzah 68
Shulchan-Orech - The Festive Mea 70
IIsrael in Education 72
Tzafun - The Afikoman 74
Barech - Blessing After the Meal 76
Hallel - Praise to G-d 80
Nirtzah - Conclusion of the Seder 84
Songs 86
Appendix – Israeli Recipes 96

The Seder Plate

Maror
a bitter vegetable, usually horseradish or lettuce

Zero'a
typically a lamb shank bone, often substituted for cooked chicken

Beitzah
a hard-boiled egg

Charoset
a sweet paste made with apples and nuts

Karpas
a green leafy vegetable, usually parsley or celery

Hazeret
more of the same or a different bitter vegetable

Matzah
beside the seder plate, we place three whole matzahs, which will play an important part in the seder

Kadesh

קַדֵּשׁ

Blessing on the Wine

Pour everyone a first full cup of wine.

 Recite the Kiddush blessing, adding the parentheses when the Seder falls on the Sabbath:

וַיְהִי עֶרֶב וַיְהִי בֹקֶר יוֹם הַשִּׁשִּׁי. וַיְכֻלּוּ הַשָּׁמַיִם וְהָאָרֶץ וְכָל צְבָאָם. וַיְכַל אֱלֹהִים בַּיּוֹם הַשְּׁבִיעִי מְלַאכְתּוֹ אֲשֶׁר עָשָׂה וַיִּשְׁבֹּת בַּיּוֹם הַשְּׁבִיעִי מִכָּל מְלַאכְתּוֹ אֲשֶׁר עָשָׂה. וַיְבָרֶךְ אֱלֹהִים אֶת יוֹם הַשְּׁבִיעִי וַיְקַדֵּשׁ אוֹתוֹ כִּי בוֹ שָׁבַת מִכָּל מְלַאכְתּוֹ אֲשֶׁר בָּרָא אֱלֹהִים לַעֲשׂוֹת.

Vayehi erev, vayehi voker, yom ha-shishi. V'yechulu ha-sha-mayim v'ha'aretz v'chol tze-va'am. V'yechal Elohim ba-yom ha-shevi'i mi-kol melachto asher asah, v'yishbot ba-yom ha-shvi'i mi-kol melachto asher asah. V'yevarech Elohim et yom ha-shvi'i v'yekadesh oto, ki vo shavat mi-kol melachto asher bara Elohim la'asot.

And so it was evening, and so it was morning, the sixth day. And G-d had completed the skies and the earth and all their host. And on the seventh day, G-d finished His work which He had done, and on the seventh day G-d rested from the work which He had done. And G-d blessed the seventh day and sanctified it, for on that day He rested from His work and all that He had done.

בָּרוּךְ אַתָּה יְיָ אֱלֹהֵינוּ מֶלֶךְ הָעוֹלָם בּוֹרֵא פְּרִי הַגָּפֶן.

Baruch atah Adonai, Eloheinu melech ha-olam, borei peri ha-gafen.

Blessed are You, Lord our G-d, King of the universe, creator of the fruit of the vine.

בָּרוּךְ אַתָּה יְיָ אֱלֹהֵינוּ מֶלֶךְ הָעוֹלָם, אֲשֶׁר בָּחַר בָּנוּ מִכָּל עָם וְרוֹמְמָנוּ מִכָּל לָשׁוֹן וְקִדְּשָׁנוּ בְּמִצְוֹתָיו. וַתִּתֶּן לָנוּ יְיָ אֱלֹהֵינוּ בְּאַהֲבָה (בְּשַׁבָּת: שַׁבָּתוֹת לִמְנוּחָה וּ) מוֹעֲדִים לְשִׂמְחָה, חַגִּים וּזְמַנִּים לְשָׂשׂוֹן, אֶת יוֹם (הַשַּׁבָּת הַזֶּה וְאֶת יוֹם) חַג הַמַּצּוֹת הַזֶּה, זְמַן חֵרוּתֵנוּ (בְּאַהֲבָה), מִקְרָא קֹדֶשׁ, זֵכֶר לִיצִיאַת מִצְרָיִם. כִּי בָנוּ בָחַרְתָּ וְאוֹתָנוּ קִדַּשְׁתָּ מִכָּל הָעַמִּים, (וְשַׁבָּת) וּמוֹעֲדֵי קָדְשֶׁךָ (בְּאַהֲבָה וּבְרָצוֹן,) בְּשִׂמְחָה וּבְשָׂשׂוֹן הִנְחַלְתָּנוּ. בָּרוּךְ אַתָּה יְיָ, מְקַדֵּשׁ (הַשַּׁבָּת וְ)יִשְׂרָאֵל וְהַזְּמַנִּים.

Baruch atah Adonai, Eloheinu melech ha-olam, asher bachar banu mi-kol 'am v'romemanu mi-kol lashon v'kideshanu b'mitzvotav. V'titen lanu Adonai Eloheinu b'ahava (shabbatot li-mnucha v') mo'adim l'-simcha, chagim uzmanim l'sason, et yom (ha-shabbat hazeh ve'et yom) chag ha-matzot hazeh, zman cheruteinu (b'ahava) mikra kodesh, Zecher l'yetziyat mitzrayim. Ki banu bacharta v'otanu kidashta mi-kol ha-amim, (v'shabbat) umo'adei kodshecha (b'ahava uvratzon,) b'simcha uvsason hinchaltanu. Baruch atah Adonai, mekadesh (ha-shabbat v') Yisrael v'ha-zmanim.

Blessed are you, Lord our G-d, King of the universe, who has chosen us among all people and raised us above all languages, and sanctified us through His commandments. The Lord our G-d has lovingly given us (the Shabbat to rest, and) festivals to be joyful, holidays and special times for gladness, this (Shabbat day and this) Passover, our time of (loving) freedom, in holiness and in memory of the Exodus from Egypt. For us You have chosen and us You have sanctified from all the people, and You have (lovingly and willingly) given us (Shabbat and) the holy times for happiness and joy. Blessed are You, G-d, who sanctifies (the Shabbat and) the people of Israel and the festivities.

On Saturday evening, add:

בָּרוּךְ אַתָּה יְיָ אֱלֹהֵינוּ מֶלֶךְ הָעוֹלָם, בּוֹרֵא מְאוֹרֵי הָאֵשׁ.

Baruch atah Adonai, Eloheinu melech ha-olam, borei me'orei ha-esh.

Blessed are You, Lord our G-d, King of the universe, creator of the light of fire.

בָּרוּךְ אַתָּה יְיָ אֱלֹהֵינוּ מֶלֶךְ הָעוֹלָם הַמַּבְדִּיל בֵּין קֹדֶשׁ לְחֹל, בֵּין אוֹר לְחֹשֶׁךְ, בֵּין יִשְׂרָאֵל לָעַמִּים, בֵּין יוֹם הַשְּׁבִיעִי לְשֵׁשֶׁת יְמֵי הַמַּעֲשֶׂה. בֵּין קְדֻשַּׁת שַׁבָּת לִקְדֻשַּׁת יוֹם טוֹב הִבְדַּלְתָּ, וְאֶת יוֹם הַשְּׁבִיעִי מִשֵּׁשֶׁת יְמֵי הַמַּעֲשֶׂה קִדַּשְׁתָּ. הִבְדַּלְתָּ וְקִדַּשְׁתָּ אֶת עַמְּךָ יִשְׂרָאֵל בִּקְדֻשָּׁתֶךָ. בָּרוּךְ אַתָּה יְיָ הַמַּבְדִּיל בֵּין קֹדֶשׁ לְקֹדֶשׁ.

Baruch atah Adonai, Eloheinu melech ha-olam, ha-mavdil beyn kodesh le-chol, beyn or le-choshech, beyn Israel l'amim, beyn yom ha-shvi'i l'sheshet yemey ha-ma'aseh. Beyn kedushat shabbat l'kedushat yom tov hivdalta, v'et yom ha-shvi'i mi-sheshet yemey ha-ma'aseh kidashta. Hivdalta v'kidashta et amcha Yisrael b'kdushatcha. Baruch atah Adonai ha-mavdil beyn kodesh l'kodesh.

Blessed are You, Lord our G-d, King of the universe, who makes a distinction between the holy and the profane, between light and darkness, between the people of Israel and the nations, between the seventh day and the six days of work. You have made the distinction between the sanctity of Shabbat and the sanctity of the holy day, and sanctified the seventh day of the six days of work. You have set apart and sanctified Your people of Israel with Your holiness. Blessed are You, G-d, who differentiates between the holy and the holy.

On the first Seder night, add:

בָּרוּךְ אַתָּה יְיָ אֱלֹהֵינוּ מֶלֶךְ הָעוֹלָם, שֶׁהֶחֱיָנוּ וְקִיְּמָנוּ וְהִגִּיעָנוּ לַזְּמַן הַזֶּה.

Baruch atah Adonai, Eloheinu melech ha-olam, sh'hecheyanu v'kiyemanu v'higiyanu l'zman hazeh.

Blessed are You, Lord our G-d, King of the universe, who has given us life, sustained us, and allowed us to reach this time.

 Drink the first cup of wine.

Urchatz

וּרְחַץ

Washing Hands

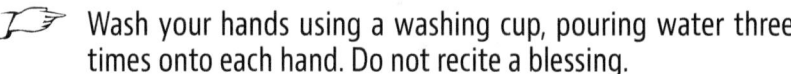 Wash your hands using a washing cup, pouring water three times onto each hand. Do not recite a blessing.

Israel in Progressiveness

Golda Meir – Female Prime Minister

When Kyiv-born Golda Meir was elected as Israel's fourth Prime Minister in 1969, she was only the world's third elected female state leader in modern times. Meir's election put Israel lightyears ahead of other Western countries, many of which, to this very day, have yet to elect a female leader. Meir was known for being firm, resolute, and an unapologetic Zionist.

LGBTQ+ in Israel

Tel Aviv is commonly dubbed the "Gay Capital of the Middle East," and rightfully so. While neighboring states fall far behind in the rights they allow people who identify as LGBTQ+, in Israel, year after year, legislations are passed to improve queer people's overall lifestyle and their equality in society. Israel even grants asylum to members of the LGBTQ+ community living in areas under the jurisdiction of the Palestinian Authority, where there is often violent punishment of sexual minorities.

Humanitarian Aid

Among the community of nations, Israel is most often the first to lend a hand when natural disasters hit worldwide. Israeli military and civilian delegations have responded to countless earthquakes, tsunamis, hurricanes, and other natural disasters, offering their know-how, aid, and professionals to anyone in need. There are even designated units in the IDF's Homefront Command intended exactly for these sorts of aid missions.

Social Equality

Israel practices complete social equality, including protecting women's rights, freedom of religion, and granting equal rights to all citizens, Jewish or otherwise. Abortion in Israel is legal, people of all races and religions serve in the IDF and government, and same-sex marriages are recognized by the legal system. In fact, Israel is the only country in the Middle Easy with a growing number of Christian citizens.

Did you know?

Israel is the only country in the world with mandatory military service for women. Women serve in all branches of the IDF – from combat and intelligence to air force and logistics

Karpas

כַּרְפַּס

The Leafy Vegetable

☞ Take some karpas (parsley, celery, or another leafy green vegetable) and dip it into salt water.

📜 Recite the blessing:

בָּרוּךְ אַתָּה יְיָ אֱלֹהֵינוּ מֶלֶךְ הָעוֹלָם, בּוֹרֵא פְּרִי הָאֲדָמָה.

Baruch atah Adonai, Eloheinu Melech ha-olam, borei peri ha-adama.

Blessed are You, Lord our G-d, King of the universe, creator of the fruit of the earth.

☞ After reciting the blessing, eat the karpas.

Yachatz

יַחַץ

Breaking
the Middle Matzah

☞ Of the three matzahs we put aside at the start of the Seder, take the middle one and break it into two. Don't try to break it perfectly in half, as we want to have one piece bigger than the other.

☞ Take the larger piece and set it aside. This will be our Afikoman. It is customary for the leader of the seder to hide the Afikoman during the Seder for younger participants to find.

☞ Return the smaller piece to its place between the first and third matzahs.

Israel in High-Tech

Start-Up Culture

Known to many as "The Start-Up Nation," Israel places third in the world for number of start-ups per capita, as well as venture capital availability. Israeli start-ups have been bought in some of the world's biggest acquisition deals and continue to shine with promise. Most of Israel's start-up culture is centralized to Tel Aviv, although growing tech and business centers across the country are contributing to a greater, more diverse ecosystem.

Waze

Waze, an Israeli-developed navigation app, has transformed the way people navigate the roads with its innovative, user-driven approach. Waze utilizes crowdsourced data to allow users to contribute information directly, enhancing the accuracy and reliability of its navigation services. This demonstrates Israel's leadership in creating groundbreaking digital solutions that address everyday challenges.

Intel

Intel Israel changed the face of technology when it invented the 8088 processor, a groundbreaking innovation built to improve computer processing, which is considered one of the global company's most significant milestones.

Wix

Wix is a leading Israeli company that has revolutionized web development with its user-friendly website building platform. Its drag-and-drop interface, coupled with a wide range of customizable templates and features, allows users to design and manage their own websites easily. With Wix, companies and individuals can create professional-looking websites without the need for extensive coding knowledge, or any at all.

Did you know?

Israel is the only country in the world (yet) where the Starbucks coffee chain failed to gain popularity. Israelis love their authentic coffee and were unimpressed, leading all six Tel Aviv branches to close within three years of launching.

Magid

מַגִּיד

Telling the Story of Exodus

Uncover the Matzah for all to see, and raise it in the air while reciting the following:

הָא לַחְמָא עַנְיָא דִי אֲכָלוּ אַבְהָתָנָא בְּאַרְעָא דְמִצְרָיִם. כָּל דִכְפִין יֵיתֵי וְיֵיכֹל, כָּל דִצְרִיךְ יֵיתֵי וְיִפְסַח. הָשַׁתָּא הָכָא, לְשָׁנָה הַבָּאָה בְּאַרְעָא דְיִשְׂרָאֵל. הָשַׁתָּא עַבְדֵי, לְשָׁנָה הַבָּאָה בְּנֵי חוֹרִין.

Ha lachma anya, di achalu avhatana b'ar'a d'mitsrayim. Kol dichfin yetey v'yechol, kol ditsrich yetey v'yifsach. Hashata hacha, l'shana haba'a b'ara d'yisrael. Hashata avdey, l'shana haba'a bney chorin.

This is the bread of poverty that our ancestors ate in the land of Egypt. All who are hungry may come and eat, all who are in need may come and celebrate with us. Now we are here, here's to next year in the land of Israel. Now we are slaves, here's to next year as a free people.

 Put the matzah down and cover it again.

 Pour the second cup of wine.

Mah Nishtanah – What Is Different?

☞ It is traditional for the youngest participant of each Seder to ask the four questions, with the rest of the participants replying.

מַה נִּשְׁתַּנָּה הַלַּיְלָה הַזֶּה מִכָּל הַלֵּילוֹת ?	Mah nishtanah halaylah hazeh mikol haleylot?
שֶׁבְּכָל הַלֵּילוֹת אָנוּ אוֹכְלִין חָמֵץ וּמַצָּה, הַלַּיְלָה הַזֶּה - כֻּלּוֹ מַצָּה.	She-b'kol haleylot anu ochlin chametz u'matzah, halaylah hazeh – kulo matzah.
שֶׁבְּכָל הַלֵּילוֹת אָנוּ אוֹכְלִין שְׁאָר יְרָקוֹת, - הַלַּיְלָה הַזֶּה מָרוֹר.	She-b'kol haleylot anu ochlin she'ar yerakot, halaylah hazeh – maror.
שֶׁבְּכָל הַלֵּילוֹת אֵין אָנוּ מַטְבִּילִין אֲפִילוּ פַּעַם אֶחָת, - הַלַּיְלָה הַזֶּה שְׁתֵּי פְעָמִים.	She-b'kol haleylot eyn anu matbilin afilu pa'am achat, halaylah hazeh – shtey pe'amim.
שֶׁבְּכָל הַלֵּילוֹת אָנוּ אוֹכְלִין בֵּין יוֹשְׁבִין וּבֵין מְסֻבִּין, - הַלַּיְלָה הַזֶּה כֻּלָּנוּ מְסֻבִּין.	She-b'kol haleylot anu ochlin beynyoshvin u'beyn mesubin, halaylah hazeh – kulanu mesubin.

What makes this night different from any other night?

On every other night we eat chametz and matzah. On this night – only matzah.

On every other night we eat all kinds of vegetables. On this night – only maror.

On every other night we do not dip our vegetables even once. On this night – we dip twice.

On every other night we eat reclining and sitting straight. On this night – we all recline.

עֲבָדִים הָיִינוּ לְפַרְעֹה בְּמִצְרָיִם, וַיּוֹצִיאֵנוּ יְיָ אֱלֹהֵינוּ מִשָּׁם בְּיָד חֲזָקָה וּבִזְרוֹעַ נְטוּיָה. וְאִלּוּ לֹא הוֹצִיא הַקָּדוֹשׁ בָּרוּךְ הוּא אֶת אֲבוֹתֵינוּ מִמִּצְרַיִם, הֲרֵי אָנוּ וּבָנֵינוּ וּבְנֵי בָנֵינוּ מְשֻׁעְבָּדִים הָיִינוּ לְפַרְעֹה בְּמִצְרָיִם.

Avadim hayinu l'paroh b'mitsrayim, v'yotsi'anu Adonai Eloheinu misham b'yad chazakah u'vizro'a netuya. V'ilu lo hotzi ha-Kadosh Baruch Hu et avoteynu m'mitsrayim, harey anu u'vaneynu u'vney vaneynu meshu'abadim hayinu l'paroh b'mitsrayim

We were slaves of Pharoah in Egypt, until the Lord our G-d took us out from there with a strong hand and an outstretched arm. Had G-d, blessed be His name, not liberated our ancestors from Egypt, we and our sons and daughters and their sons and daughters would still be enslaved to Pharoah in Egypt today.

אֲפִילוּ כֻּלָּנוּ חֲכָמִים, כֻּלָּנוּ נְבוֹנִים, כֻּלָּנוּ זְקֵנִים, כֻּלָּנוּ יוֹדְעִים אֶת הַתּוֹרָה, מִצְוָה עָלֵינוּ לְסַפֵּר בִּיצִיאַת מִצְרַיִם. וְכָל הַמַּרְבֶּה לְסַפֵּר בִּיצִיאַת מִצְרַיִם הֲרֵי זֶה מְשֻׁבָּח.

V'afilu kulanu chachamim, kulanu nevonim, kulanu zkenim, kulanu yod'im et ha-torah, mitzvah aleynu lesaper b'yetsiat mitsrayim. V'chol hamarbeh lesaper b'yetsiat mitsrayim, harey zeh meshubach.

And although we are all intelligent, wise, learned, we all know the torah, we are commanded to tell the story of the Exodus from Egypt. And the more we tell the story, the better.

Did you know?

Around 43% of the world's Jewish population resides in Israel, with many more visiting regularly and calling Israel a second home. Since its establishment, Jews from every corner of the world have been welcomed to Israel with open arms.

מַעֲשֶׂה בְּרַבִּי אֱלִיעֶזֶר וְרַבִּי יְהוֹשֻׁעַ וְרַבִּי אֶלְעָזָר בֶּן עֲזַרְיָה וְרַבִּי עֲקִיבָא וְרַבִּי טַרְפוֹן שֶׁהָיוּ מְסֻבִּין בִּבְנֵי בְרַק, וְהָיוּ מְסַפְּרִים בִּיצִיאַת מִצְרַיִם כָּל אוֹתוֹ הַלַּיְלָה עַד שֶׁבָּאוּ תַלְמִידֵיהֶם וְאָמְרוּ לָהֶם: רַבּוֹתֵינוּ, הִגִּיעַ זְמַן קְרִיאַת שְׁמַע שֶׁל שַׁחֲרִית.

Ma'aseh b'rabi Eliezer v'rabi Yehoshua v'rabi Elazar ben azaryah v'rabi akiva v'rabi tardon she-hayu mesubin bi-vney beraq, v'hayu mesaprim b'yetzi'at mitzrayim kol oto ha'laylah ad she-ba'u talmid-eyhem v'amru lahem: rabo-teynu, higiya zeman kriyat shema shel shacharit.

A story is told of Rabbi Eliezer and Rabbi Yehoshua and Rabbi Elazar Ben Azaryah and Rabbi Akiva and Rabbk Tarfon, who resided in Benei Beraq, and told the story of the exodus from Egypt all that night. Until their students came to them and told them: our teachers, it is time to say the shema for the morning prayer.

Did you know?

Over one million notes are left between the cracks of the Western Wall in Jerusalem each year, most addressed directly to God. People will visit the historic site to share their deepest hopes, wishes, and gratitude at what is considered one of the most religiously significant places on Earth.

Israel in Innovation

SodaStream

SodaStream has transformed the way consumers make carbonated beverages at home. The company's home soda machines allow users to carbonate water and create a variety of flavored drinks using reusable bottles and syrups, significantly reducing single-use plastic waste. Acquired by PepsiCo in 2018, SodaStream continues to lead the way in promoting sustainability and providing a convenient, cost-effective alternative to bottled carbonated drinks.

Uzi

The Uzi submachine gun, which has been widely used in global military combat, was one of the first weapons to incorporate a telescoping bolt, an innovative design which allows for a lighter, shorter weapon. The Uzi was developed by an IDF Major in Israel's early years and came to be a staple of modern warfare.

Rav Bariach

Rav-Bariach was established in 1873 and quickly rose to fame as a leading pioneer of home security. The company's patented steel security doors were a global gamechanger, and have continued to set the standard for strength, durability, and safety for decades.

Hetz Anti-Ballistic Missile

The "Hetz", or in English, the Arrow, is a key component of Israel's advanced missile defense system. Developed jointly by Israel Aerospace Industries (IAI) and the U.S. defense contractor Boeing, the Hetz system is designed to intercept and destroy incoming ballistic missiles at high altitudes before they can reach their targets. Israel manufactures and distributes this technology worldwide, allowing other countries to improve their security systems and keep their citizens safer.The Four Children

Did you know?

Thirteen Israelis have won Nobel Prizes, a staggering number considering its under-10,000,000 population and its having been a state for a mere 70 years. Israeli Nobel Prizes have been awarded for achievements in Chemistry, Economics, Literature, and Peace.

כְּנֶגֶד אַרְבָּעָה בָנִים דִּבְּרָה תוֹרָה. אֶחָד חָכָם, וְאֶחָד רָשָׁע, וְאֶחָד תָּם, וְאֶחָד שֶׁאֵינוֹ יוֹדֵעַ לִשְׁאוֹל.

Ke-neged arba'ah banim di-brah torah. Echad chacham, v'echad rasha, v'echad tam, v'eched she'eyno yode'a lishol.

The Torah tells us of four children. One who is wise, one who is wicked, one who is simple, and one who does not know how to ask.

חָכָם מָה הוּא אוֹמֵר?

מָה הָעֵדוֹת וְהַחֻקִּים וְהַמִּשְׁפָּטִים אֲשֶׁר צִוָּה יְיָ אֱלֹהֵינוּ אֶתְכֶם? וְאַף אַתָּה אֱמָר לוֹ כְּהִלְכוֹת הַפֶּסַח: אֵין מַפְטִירִין אַחַר הַפֶּסַח אֲפִיקוֹמָן.

Chacham ma hu omer?

Me ha-edot v'ha-hukim v'ha-mishpatim asher tsivah Adonai Eloheynu etchem?

V'af atah emor lo k'hilchot ha'pesach: eyn maftirin ahar ha-pesach afikoman.

The wise one, what does he say?

"What are these rules and rituals that the Lord our G-d has commanded you?"

And you shall tell him all about the rituals of Passover up until the very last rule, that we do not eat anything else after the Afikoman.

רָשָׁע מָה הוּא אוֹמֵר?
מָה הָעֲבֹדָה הַזֹּאת לָכֶם?
לָכֶם - וְלֹא לוֹ. וּלְפִי שֶׁהוֹצִיא אֶת עַצְמוֹ מִן הַכְּלָל כָּפַר בָּעִקָּר. וְאַף אַתָּה הַקְהֵה אֶת שִׁנָּיו וֶאֱמֹר לוֹ: בַּעֲבוּר זֶה עָשָׂה יְיָ לִי בְּצֵאתִי מִמִּצְרָיִם. לִי - וְלֹא לוֹ. אִילּוּ הָיָה שָׁם, לֹא הָיָה נִגְאָל.

Rasha ma hu omer?
Me ha'avoda hazot lachem?
Lachem- v'lo lo. U'lefi she-hotsi et atsmo min ha-klal kafar ba-ikar. V'af atah hakheh et shi-nav v'emor lo: ba'avur ze asah Adonai li b'tseyti m'mitsrayim. Li- v'lo lo. Ilu hayah sham, lo hayah nigal.

The wicked one, what does he say?

"What are these rules you follow?"

You – and not he. By excluding himself from his people, he denies the foundation of Passover. You shall tell him: It is because of what G-d did for me when I was liberated from Egypt. Me, and not him. Had he been there, he would not have been freed.

תָּם מָה הוּא אוֹמֵר?
מַה זֹּאת?
וְאָמַרְתָּ אֵלָיו: בְּחֹזֶק יָד הוֹצִיאָנוּ יְיָ מִמִּצְרַיִם, מִבֵּית עֲבָדִים.

Tam ma hu omer?
"Ma zot?"
V'amarta eylav: b'chozek yad hotzi'anu Adonai m'mitzrayim, mi-beyt avadim.

The simple one, what does he say?

"What's all this?"

And you shall say to him: G-d liberated us with a mighty hand from Egypt and from slavery.

וְשֶׁאֵינוֹ יוֹדֵעַ לִשְׁאוֹל - אַתְּ פְּתַח לוֹ, שֶׁנֶּאֱמַר: וְהִגַּדְתָּ לְבִנְךָ בַּיּוֹם הַהוּא לֵאמֹר, בַּעֲבוּר זֶה עָשָׂה יְיָ לִי בְּצֵאתִי מִמִּצְרָיִם.

V'she-eyno yode'a lishol – at petach lo, she-ne'emar: v'higadta l'vincha be-yom hahu l'eymor, ba'avur ze asah Adonai li b'tsyeti m'mitsrayim.

And the one who does not know how to ask, you shall tell him the story yourself, as it is said: tell your child on that day, it is because of what G-d did for me when I came out of Egypt.

☞ Raise your full cup of wine and say together:

וְהִיא שֶׁעָמְדָה לַאֲבוֹתֵינוּ וְלָנוּ.
שֶׁלֹּא אֶחָד בִּלְבָד עָמַד עָלֵינוּ
לְכַלּוֹתֵנוּ, אֶלָּא שֶׁבְּכָל דּוֹר וָדוֹר
עוֹמְדִים עָלֵינוּ לְכַלּוֹתֵנוּ, וְהַקָּדוֹשׁ
בָּרוּךְ הוּא מַצִּילֵנוּ מִיָּדָם.

V'hi she-amda l'avoteynu v'lanu. She-lo echad bilvad amad aleynu l'chaloteinu, ela she-b'chol dor v'dor, omdim aleynu l'chaloteinu, v'ha-Kadosh Baruch Hu matsiley-nu m'yadam.

This promise has been upheld for our ancestors and for us.

For over the years, every generation, there have been those who have wanted to defeat and annihilate us, and G-d, Blessed be His Name, has saved us from them time and time again.

 Put down the cup of wine.

Did you know?

The Dead Sea in Israel is the lowest aboveground point on the globe, located at 1,315 feet below sea level. An especially impressive feat, seeing as it is only 50 miles away from the closest coast.

Did you know?

Israel is the only country in the world to see a positive increase in the number of its trees since the start of the 21st century. Each year, Israelis celebrate Tu B'Shvat, "New Year of the Trees", by going out and planting trees all over the country.

The Ten Plagues

אֵלוּ עֶשֶׂר מַכּוֹת שֶׁהֵבִיא הַקָּדוֹשׁ בָּרוּךְ הוּא עַל הַמִּצְרִים בְּמִצְרָיִם, וְאֵלוּ הֵן:

Eylu eser ha-makot she-hevi ha-Kadosh Baruch Hu al ha-mitsrim b'mitsrayim, v'eylu hen:

These are the ten plagues that G-d, Blessed be His Name, brought down upon the Egyptians in Egypt:

 As you recite the ten plagues, pour a drop of wine from your cup onto a plate for each.

דָּם Dam **Blood**

צְפַרְדֵּעַ Tsfardeya **Frogs**

כִּנִּים Kinim **Lice**

עָרוֹב Arov **Wild Beasts**

דֶּבֶר Dever **Plague**

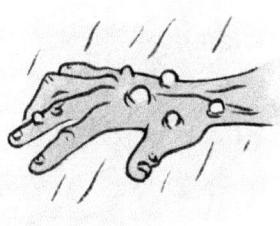

שְׁחִין Shechin **Boils**

בָּרָד Barad **Hail**

אַרְבֶּה Arbeh **Locusts**

חֹשֶׁךְ Choshech **Darkness**

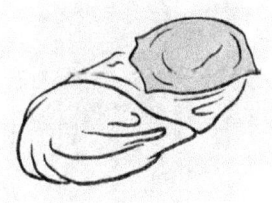

מַכַּת בְּכוֹרוֹת Makat Bechorot
Slaying of the Firstborn

רַבִּי יְהוּדָה הָיָה נוֹתֵן בָּהֶם סִמָּנִים:

Rabi Yehudah hayah noten bahem simanim:

Rabbi Yehuda would assign them mnemonics:

דְּצַ"ךְ   Detsach (blood, frogs, lice)

עֲדַ"שׁ   Adash (wild beasts, plague, boils)

בְּאַחַ"ב   B'achav (hail, locusts, darkness, slaying of the firstborn)

 Pour another drop of wine for each of the three mnemonics.

 Remove the cup of wine and the plate with the wine you spilled and refill your second cup of wine.

רַבִּי יוֹסֵי הַגְּלִילִי אוֹמֵר: מִנַּיִן אַתָּה אוֹמֵר שֶׁלָּקוּ הַמִּצְרִים בְּמִצְרַיִם עֶשֶׂר מַכּוֹת וְעַל הַיָּם לָקוּ חֲמִשִּׁים מַכּוֹת?

בְּמִצְרַיִם מָה הוּא אוֹמֵר? וַיֹּאמְרוּ הַחַרְטֻמִּים אֶל פַּרְעֹה: אֶצְבַּע אֱלֹהִים הִוא, וְעַל הַיָּם מָה הוּא אוֹמֵר? וַיַּרְא יִשְׂרָאֵל אֶת הַיָּד הַגְּדֹלָה אֲשֶׁר עָשָׂה יְיָ בְּמִצְרַיִם, וַיִּירְאוּ הָעָם אֶת יְיָ, וַיַּאֲמִינוּ בַּיְיָ וּבְמֹשֶׁה עַבְדּוֹ. כַּמָּה לָקוּ בְאֶצְבַּע? עֶשֶׂר מַכּוֹת. אֱמוֹר מֵעַתָּה: בְּמִצְרַיִם לָקוּ עֶשֶׂר מַכּוֹת וְעַל הַיָּם לָקוּ חֲמִשִּׁים מַכּוֹת.

Rabi Yosey ha-glili omer: mi-nay-in atah omer she-laku ha-mitz-rim b'mitzrayim eser makot v'al ha-yam laku chamishim makot?

B'mitzrayim ma hu omer? Va-yomru ha-chartumim el paroh: etsba Elohim hi, v'al ha-yam me hu omer? Va-yar Yisrael et ha-yad ha-gedolah asher asa Adonay b'mitsrayim, va-yiru ha-am et Adonay, va-ya'aminu b'Adonay u'v'moshe avdo. Kama laku v'etsba? Eser makot. Emor me'ata: b'mitsrayim laku eser makot v'al ha-yam laku chamishim makot.

Rabbi Yossey of the Galillei would ask: how do we know that the Egyptians were struck by ten plagues in Egypt and fifty plagues at sea?

In Egypt, what does it say? And the magicians said to Pharaoh: it is the hand of G-d. And at sea, what does it say? And Israel saw the mighty hand that G-d swept upon Egypt, and they feared G-d and trusted in Him and in Moses, his servant. Hoy many were they struck by the hand? Ten plagues. Thus, you shall say from now on: In Egypt they were struck by ten plagues and at sea they were struck by fifty plagues.

רַבִּי אֱלִיעֶזֶר אוֹמֵר: מִנַּיִן שֶׁכָּל מַכָּה וּמַכָּה שֶׁהֵבִיא הַקָּדוֹשׁ בָּרוּךְ הוּא עַל הַמִּצְרִים בְּמִצְרַיִם הָיְתָה שֶׁל אַרְבַּע מַכּוֹת?

שֶׁנֶּאֱמַר: יְשַׁלַּח בָּם חֲרוֹן אַפּוֹ, עֶבְרָה וָזַעַם וְצָרָה, מִשְׁלַחַת מַלְאֲכֵי רָעִים. עֶבְרָה – אַחַת, וָזַעַם – שְׁתַּיִם, וְצָרָה – שָׁלשׁ, מִשְׁלַחַת מַלְאֲכֵי רָעִים – אַרְבַּע. אֱמוֹר מֵעַתָּה: בְּמִצְרַיִם לָקוּ אַרְבָּעִים מַכּוֹת וְעַל הַיָּם לָקוּ מָאתַיִם מַכּוֹת.

Rabi Eliezer omer: mi-nayin she-kol makah v'makah she-hevi ha-Kadosh Baruch Hu al ha-mitsrim b'mitsrayim haytah shel arba makot?

She-ne'emar: yishlach bahem charon apo, evrah v'za'am v'tsarah, mishlachat mal'achei ra'im. Evra – achat, v'za'am – shtayim, v'tsarah – shalosh, mishlachat mal'achei ra'im – arba. Emor me-atah: b'mitsrayim laku arba'im makot v'al ha-yam laku matayim makot.

Rabbi Eliezer would ask: how do we know that each plague inflicted by G-d on the Egyptians in Egypt was worth four plagues?

It is said: and he unleashed upon them his rage, anger and wrath and troubles, a delegation of messengers of evil. Anger – is one, wrath – makes two, troubles – make three, and messengers of evil make four. Thus, you shall say from now on: In Egypt they were struck by forty plagues, and at sea they were struck by two hundred plagues.

רַבִּי עֲקִיבָא אוֹמֵר: מִנַּיִן שֶׁכָּל מַכָּה וּמַכָּה שֶׁהֵבִיא הַקָּדוֹשׁ בָּרוּךְ הוּא עַל הַמִּצְרִים בְּמִצְרַיִם הָיְתָה שֶׁל חָמֵשׁ מַכּוֹת?

שֶׁנֶּאֱמַר: יְשַׁלַּח בָּם חֲרוֹן אַפּוֹ, עֶבְרָה וָזַעַם וְצָרָה, מִשְׁלַחַת מַלְאֲכֵי רָעִים. חֲרוֹן אַפּוֹ - אַחַת, עֶבְרָה - שְׁתַּיִם, וָזַעַם - שָׁלֹשׁ, וְצָרָה - אַרְבַּע, מִשְׁלַחַת מַלְאֲכֵי רָעִים - חָמֵשׁ. אֱמוֹר מֵעַתָּה: בְּמִצְרַיִם לָקוּ חֲמִשִּׁים מַכּוֹת וְעַל הַיָּם לָקוּ חֲמִשִּׁים וּמָאתַיִם מַכּוֹת.

Rabi Akiva omer: mi-nayin she-kol makah v'makah she-hevi ha-Kadosh Baruch Hu al ha-mitsrim b'mitsrayim hayta shel chamesh makot?

She-ne'emar: yishlach bam charon apo, evrah v'za'am v'tsarah, mishlachat mal'achei ra'im. Charon apo – achat, evra – shtayim, v'za'am – shalosh, v'tsarah – arba, mishlachat mal'achei ra'im – chamesh. Emor me-atah: b'mitsrayim laku chamishim makot v'al ha-yam laku chamishim u'matay-im makot.

Rabbi Akiva would ask: how do we know that each plague inflicted by G-d on the Egyptians in Egypt was worth five plagues?

It is said: and he unleashed upon them his rage, anger and wrath and troubles, a delegation of messengers of evil. Rage – is one, anger – makes two, wrath – makes three, troubles – make four, and messengers of evil make five. Thus, you shall say from now on: In Egypt they were struck by fifty plagues, and at sea they were struck by fifty and two hundred plagues.

Israel in Culture

Infected Mushroom

Musical duo "Infected Mushroom", formed by Erez Eisen and Amit Duvdevani, is one of the most prominent and influential groups in the electronic music scene. Their early albums quickly gained popularity for their fast tempos, complex melodies, and layered textures, and their music is played today at parties and festivals everywhere in the world. The two are known for their particularly lively performances, which they deliver internationally.

Rummikub

You may not have known that the popular number tile game, a classic in any household, was actually developed by Ephraim Hertzano, one of the many Jews to immigrate to the new state of Israel from Romania after World War II. Hertzano hand-made the first Rummikub sets, which became international bestsellers in no time.

Shenkar Engineering and Design College

Shenkar School of Engineering & Design is widely acknowledged as one of the world's leading art schools, turning out renowned designers and winning countless prestigious awards. Located in the suburbs of Tel Aviv, Shenkar college's uniqueness lies in its multidisciplinary approach and cutting-edge technology.

Israeli Street Food

Israeli street food is beloved worldwide for its vibrant flavors, fresh ingredients, and diverse culinary traditions. Iconic dishes like falafel, hummus, shawarma, and sabich have found their way onto menus in cities across the globe, reflecting a growing appreciation for the rich and diverse food culture of Israel. Celebrity chefs like Yotam Ottolenghi and Eyal Shani have played a significant role in the popularity of Israeli cuisine.

Did you know?

Until its revival from extinction in the 19th century, Hebrew was considered a dead language – one that had not been spoken outside of religious context for centuries. Today, it is one of the official languages of Israel, alongside Arabic.

Dayeinu

כַּמָּה מַעֲלוֹת טוֹבוֹת לַמָּקוֹם עָלֵינוּ!

Kama ma'alot tovot la-makom aleynu!

אִלּוּ הוֹצִיאָנוּ מִמִּצְרַיִם וְלֹא עָשָׂה בָהֶם שְׁפָטִים, דַּיֵּינוּ.

Ilu hotsi'anu m'mitsrayim v'lo asah vahem shefatim, dayeinu.

אִלּוּ עָשָׂה בָהֶם שְׁפָטִים, וְלֹא עָשָׂה בֵאלֹהֵיהֶם, דַּיֵּינוּ.

Ilu asah behm shefatim v'lo asah b'eloheyhem, dayeinu.

אִלּוּ עָשָׂה בֵאלֹהֵיהֶם, וְלֹא הָרַג אֶת בְּכוֹרֵיהֶם, דַּיֵּינוּ.

Ilu asah b'eloheyhem v'lo harag et bechoreyhem, dayeinu.

אִלּוּ הָרַג אֶת בְּכוֹרֵיהֶם וְלֹא נָתַן לָנוּ אֶת מָמוֹנָם, דַּיֵּינוּ.

Ilu harag et bechoreyhem v'lo natan lanu et mamonam, dayeinu.

אִלּוּ נָתַן לָנוּ אֶת מָמוֹנָם וְלֹא קָרַע לָנוּ אֶת הַיָּם, דַּיֵּינוּ.

Ilu natan lanu et mamonam v'lo kara lanu et hayam, dayeinu.

אִלּוּ קָרַע לָנוּ אֶת הַיָּם וְלֹא הֶעֱבִירָנוּ בְתוֹכוֹ בֶּחָרָבָה, דַּיֵּינוּ.

Ilu kara lanu et hayam v'lo he'eyviranu betocho b'charavah, dayeinu.

אִלּוּ הֶעֱבִירָנוּ בְתוֹכוֹ בֶּחָרָבָה וְלֹא שִׁקַּע צָרֵנוּ בְּתוֹכוֹ, דַּיֵּינוּ.

Ilu he'eyviranu betocho b'charavah v'lo shika tsareynu betocho, dayeinu.

אִלּוּ שִׁקַּע צָרֵנוּ בְּתוֹכוֹ וְלֹא סִפֵּק צָרְכֵּנוּ בַּמִּדְבָּר אַרְבָּעִים שָׁנָה, דַּיֵּינוּ.

Ilu shika tsareynu betocho v'lo sipek tsarcheynu ba-midbar arba'im shanah, dayeinu.

אִלּוּ סִפֵּק צָרְכֵּנוּ בַּמִּדְבָּר אַרְבָּעִים שָׁנָה וְלֹא הֶאֱכִילָנוּ אֶת הַמָּן, דַּיֵּינוּ.

Ilu sipek tsarcheynu ba-midbar arba'im shanah v'lo he'eychilanu et ha-man, dayeinu.

Ilu he'eychilanu et ha-man v'lo natan lanu et ha-shabbat, dayeinu.	אִלּוּ הֶאֱכִילָנוּ אֶת הַמָּן וְלֹא נָתַן לָנוּ אֶת הַשַּׁבָּת, דַּיֵּנוּ.
Ilu natan lanu et ha-shabbat v'lo kervanu lifney har sinai, dayeinu.	אִלּוּ קֵרְבָנוּ לִפְנֵי הַר סִינַי, וְלֹא נָתַן לָנוּ אֶת הַתּוֹרָה, דַּיֵּנוּ.
Ilu kervanu lifney har sinai v'lo natan lanu et ha-torah, dayeinu.	אִלּוּ נָתַן לָנוּ אֶת הַשַּׁבָּת, וְלֹא קֵרְבָנוּ לִפְנֵי הַר סִינַי, דַּיֵּנוּ.
Ilu natan lanu et ha-torah v'lo hichnisanu l'eretz yisrael, dayeinu.	אִלּוּ נָתַן לָנוּ אֶת הַתּוֹרָה וְלֹא הִכְנִיסָנוּ לְאֶרֶץ יִשְׂרָאֵל, דַּיֵּנוּ.
Ilu hichnisanu l'eretz Yisrael v'lo vana lanu et beyt ha-behira, dayeinu.	אִלּוּ הִכְנִיסָנוּ לְאֶרֶץ יִשְׂרָאֵל וְלֹא בָנָה לָנוּ אֶת בֵּית הַבְּחִירָה, דַּיֵּנוּ.

How many good favors G-d has bestowed upon us!

Had He liberated us from Egypt and not carried out justice against the Egyptians, we would have been grateful enough.

Had He carried out justice against the Egyptians and not against their gods, we would have been grateful enough.

Had He carried out justice against their gods and not slain their firstborns, we would have been grateful enough.

Had He slain their firstborns and not given us their treasures, we would have been grateful enough.

Had He given us their treasures and not split the sea for us, we would have been grateful enough.

Had He split the sea for us and not let us through it on dry land, we would have been grateful enough.

Had He led us through the sea on dry land and not drowned our enemies in it, we would have been grateful enough.

Had He drowned our enemies in the sea and not provided for us in the desert for forty years, we would have been grateful enough.

Had He provided for us in the desert for forty years and not given us the manna, we would have been grateful enough.

Had He given us the manna and not given us the Sabbath, we would have been grateful enough.

Had He given us the Sabbath and not brought us to Mount Sinai, we would have been grateful enough.

Had He brought us to Mount Sinai and not given us the Torah, we would have been grateful enough.

Had He given us the Torah and not brought us into Israel, we would have been grateful enough.

Had He brought us into Israel and not built the Temple of worship, we would have been grateful enough.

עַל אַחַת, כַּמָּה וְכַמָּה, טוֹבָה כְפוּלָה וּמְכֻפֶּלֶת לַמָּקוֹם עָלֵינוּ: שֶׁהוֹצִיאָנוּ מִמִּצְרַיִם, וְעָשָׂה בָהֶם שְׁפָטִים, וְעָשָׂה בֵאלֹהֵיהֶם, וְהָרַג אֶת בְּכוֹרֵיהֶם, וְנָתַן לָנוּ אֶת מָמוֹנָם, וְקָרַע לָנוּ אֶת הַיָּם, וְהֶעֱבִירָנוּ בְתוֹכוֹ בֶּחָרָבָה, וְשִׁקַּע צָרֵנוּ בְּתוֹכוֹ, וְסִפֵּק צָרְכֵּנוּ בַּמִּדְבָּר אַרְבָּעִים שָׁנָה, וְהֶאֱכִילָנוּ אֶת הַמָּן, וְנָתַן לָנוּ אֶת הַשַּׁבָּת, וְקֵרְבָנוּ לִפְנֵי הַר סִינַי, וְנָתַן לָנוּ אֶת הַתּוֹרָה, וְהִכְנִיסָנוּ לְאֶרֶץ יִשְׂרָאֵל, וּבָנָה לָנוּ אֶת בֵּית הַבְּחִירָה לְכַפֵּר עַל כָּל עֲוֹנוֹתֵינוּ.

Al achat kama v'chama, tova kfula u'mechupelet la-makon aleynu. She-hotzi'anu mi-mits-rayim, v'asa beham shefatim, v'asa b'eloheyhem, v'harag et bechoryhem, v'natan lanu et mamonam, v'kara lanu et ha-yam, v'he'eviranu betocho b'charavah, v'shika tsareynu betocho, v'sipek tsarkeynu ba-midbar arba'im shanah, v'he'echilanu et ha-man, v'na-tan lanu et ha-shabat, v'ker-vanu lifney har sinai, v'natan lanu et ha-torah, v'hichnisanu l'eretz Yisrael, u'vana lanu et beyt ha-bechirah lechaper al kol avonoteynu.

How much good God gives us, which is doubled and tripled. He liberated us from Egypt, and carried out justice against the Egyptians, and carried out justice against their gods, and slayed their firstborns, and gave us their treasures, and split the sea for us, and led us through the sea on dry land, and drowned our enemies in the sea, and provided for us in the desert for forty years, and gave us the manna, and gave us the Sabbath, and brought us to Mount Sinai, and gave us the Torah, and brought us into Israel, and built the Temple of worship to atone for all of our sins.The Symbols of Passover

רַבָּן גַּמְלִיאֵל הָיָה אוֹמֵר: כָּל שֶׁלֹּא אָמַר שְׁלֹשָׁה דְבָרִים אֵלוּ בַּפֶּסַח, לֹא יָצָא יְדֵי חוֹבָתוֹ, וְאֵלוּ הֵן:

Raban Gamilel hayah womer: kol she-lo amar ahloshah devarim eylu ba-pesach, lo yatsa yedey chovato, v'eylu hen:

Rabbi Gamliel would say, all who have not recited these three things on Passover have not done their duty. And these things are:

☞ All say together:

פֶּסַח, מַצָּה, וּמָרוֹר.

Pesach, matzah, u'maror.

Pesach, Matzah, and Bitter Herbs.

פֶּסַח שֶׁהָיוּ אֲבוֹתֵינוּ אוֹכְלִים בִּזְמַן שֶׁבֵּית הַמִּקְדָּשׁ הָיָה קַיָּם, עַל שׁוּם מָה?

עַל שׁוּם שֶׁפָּסַח הַקָּדוֹשׁ בָּרוּךְ הוּא עַל בָּתֵּי אֲבוֹתֵינוּ בְּמִצְרַיִם, שֶׁנֶּאֱמַר: וַאֲמַרְתֶּם זֶבַח פֶּסַח הוּא לַיי, אֲשֶׁר פָּסַח עַל בָּתֵּי בְנֵי יִשְׂרָאֵל בְּמִצְרַיִם בְּנָגְפּוֹ אֶת מִצְרַיִם, וְאֶת בָּתֵּינוּ הִצִּיל, וַיִּקֹּד הָעָם וַיִּשְׁתַּחֲווּ.

Pesach she-hayu avoteynu ochlim bizman she-beyt ha-mikdash hayah kayam, al shum mah?

Al shum she-pasach ha-Kadosh Baruch Hu al batey avoteynu b'mitsrayim, she-ne'emar: v'amartem zevach pesach hu l'Adonai, asher pasach al batey bney Yisrael b'mitsrayim b'nogfo et mitsrayim, v'et bateynu hitsil, vayikod ha'am vayishtachavu.

Pesach, the sacrificial offering that our ancestors would eat while the Temple was standing. What is the meaning of it?

In memory of how G-d passed over the homes of our ancestors in Egypt, sparing them. As it is said: The Pesach is an offering to G-d, who passed over the homes of the Israelites in Egypt as He smote the Egyptians and saved our homes. And the people bowed and genuflected before Him.

Raise the matzah and say:

מַצָּה זוֹ שֶׁאָנוּ אוֹכְלִים, עַל שׁוּם מָה?

עַל שׁוּם שֶׁלֹּא הִסְפִּיק בְּצֵקָם שֶׁל אֲבוֹתֵינוּ לְהַחֲמִיץ עַד שֶׁנִּגְלָה עֲלֵיהֶם מֶלֶךְ מַלְכֵי הַמְּלָכִים, הַקָּדוֹשׁ בָּרוּךְ הוּא, וּגְאָלָם, שֶׁנֶּאֱמַר: וַיֹּאפוּ אֶת הַבָּצֵק אֲשֶׁר הוֹצִיאוּ מִמִּצְרַיִם עֻגֹת מַצּוֹת, כִּי לֹא חָמֵץ, כִּי גֹרְשׁוּ מִמִּצְרַיִם וְלֹא יָכְלוּ לְהִתְמַהְמֵהַּ, וְגַם צֵדָה לֹא עָשׂוּ לָהֶם.

Matzah zo she-anu ochlim. Al shum mah?

Al shum she-lo hispik betsekam ahel avoteynu l'hachmitz ad she-niglah aleyhem Melech malchei ha-mlachim, Ha-Kadosh Baruch Hu, u'gealam, she-ne'emar: vayofu et ha-batsek asher hotsi'u m'mitsrayim ugot matzot, ki lo chametz, ki gorshu m'mitsrayim v'lo yachlu l'hit-mahamehah, v'gam tseydah lo asu lahem.

Matzah, this unleavened bread that we eat, what is the meaning of it?

In memory of the unleavened bread that our ancestors made and did not have time to rise before the King of Kings, G-d, Blessed be His Name, appeared before them and redeemed them. It is said: and they baked the dough that they brought with them from Egypt into matzahs, because it did not rise, as they were banished from Egypt and could not delay and did not even have time to prepare provisions.

☞ Raise the maror and say:

מָרוֹר זֶה שֶׁאָנוּ אוֹכְלִים, עַל שׁוּם מָה?

עַל שׁוּם שֶׁמֵּרְרוּ הַמִּצְרִים אֶת חַיֵּי אֲבוֹתֵינוּ בְּמִצְרַיִם, שֶׁנֶּאֱמַר: וַיְמָרֲרוּ אֶת חַיֵּיהֶם בַּעֲבֹדָה קָשָׁה, בְּחֹמֶר וּבִלְבֵנִים וּבְכָל עֲבֹדָה בַּשָּׂדֶה אֵת כָּל עֲבֹדָתָם אֲשֶׁר עָבְדוּ בָהֶם בְּפָרֶךְ

Maror ze she-anu ochlim, al shum mah?

Al shum she-mereyru ham-itsrim et chayey avoteinu b'mitsrayim, she-ne'emar: vayemareru et chayeyhem b'avoda kasha, b'chomer u'vil-venim u'vechol avoda ba-sa-deh et kol avodatam asher avdu baheym b'farech

Maror, these bitter herbs that we eat, what is the meaning of it?

In memory of the bitterness that the Egyptians inflicted on the lives of our ancestors. It is said: and they made their lives bitter with hard labor, with mortar and bricks, work in the fields and every form of slavery that they forced upon them.

בְּכָל דּוֹר וָדוֹר חַיָּב אָדָם לִרְאוֹת אֶת עַצְמוֹ כְּאִלּוּ הוּא יָצָא מִמִּצְרַיִם, שֶׁנֶּאֱמַר: וְהִגַּדְתָּ לְבִנְךָ בַּיּוֹם הַהוּא לֵאמֹר, בַּעֲבוּר זֶה עָשָׂה יְיָ לִי בְּצֵאתִי מִמִּצְרָיִם.

B'chol dor va'dor chayav adam lirot et atsmo ke'ilu hu yatsa m'mitsrayim, she-ne'emar: v'higadta l'vincha bayom hahu l'emor: ba'avur ze asah Adonai li b'tseyti m'mitsrayim.

In every generation, every person must see themselves as though they had been liberated from Egypt, as it is said: and on that day, you shall tell your child all that G-d did for you when He set you free from Egypt.

לֹא אֶת אֲבוֹתֵינוּ בִּלְבָד גָּאַל הַקָּדוֹשׁ בָּרוּךְ הוּא, אֶלָּא אַף אוֹתָנוּ גָּאַל עִמָּהֶם, שֶׁנֶּאֱמַר: וְאוֹתָנוּ הוֹצִיא מִשָּׁם, לְמַעַן הָבִיא אֹתָנוּ, לָתֶת לָנוּ אֶת הָאָרֶץ אֲשֶׁר נִשְׁבַּע לַאֲבֹתֵנוּ.

Lo et avoteynu bilvad ga'al ha-Kadosh Baruch Hu, ela af otanu ga'al imahem, she-ne'emar: v'otanu hotsi mi'sham, l'ma'an hevi otanu, latet lanu et ha-aretz asher nishba l'avoteynu.

Not only our forefathers did G-d, blessed be His name, redeem, but He redeemed us alongside them, as it is said: and He removed us from there, to deliver us, to give us the land that he swore to our ancestors.

לְפִיכָךְ אֲנַחְנוּ חַיָּבִים לְהוֹדוֹת, לְהַלֵּל, לְשַׁבֵּחַ, לְפָאֵר, לְרוֹמֵם, לְהַדֵּר, לְבָרֵךְ, לְעַלֵּה וּלְקַלֵּס לְמִי שֶׁעָשָׂה לַאֲבוֹתֵינוּ וְלָנוּ אֶת כָּל הַנִּסִּים הָאֵלּוּ: הוֹצִיאָנוּ מֵעַבְדוּת לְחֵרוּת מִיָּגוֹן לְשִׂמְחָה, וּמֵאֵבֶל לְיוֹם טוֹב, וּמֵאֲפֵלָה לְאוֹר גָּדוֹל, וּמִשִּׁעְבּוּד לִגְאֻלָּה. וְנֹאמַר לְפָנָיו: הַלְלוּיָהּ.

L'fichach anachnu chayavim l'hodot, l'halel, l'shabeyach, l'fa'er, l'romem, l'hader, l'vareych, l'aleh u'l'kaleys l'mi she-asa l'avoteynu v'lanu et kol ha-nisim ha'eylu: hotsi'anu m'avdut l'cheyrut m'yagon l'simcha, u'm'eyvel l'yom tov, u'm'afeyla l'or gadol, u'm'shi'abud li-g'ula. V'nomar lefanav, halleluyah.

Therefore, we must give thanks, praise, glorify, exalt, laud, revere, bless, magnify, and extol He who did for our forefathers and for us all of these miracles: delivered us from slavery to freedom, from sorrow to joy, from grief to celebration, from darkness to light, and from subjugation to redemption. And to Him we say, hallelujah.

הַלְלוּ יָהּ הַלְלוּ עַבְדֵי יְהוָה הַלְלוּ אֶת שֵׁם יְהוָה. יְהִי שֵׁם יְהוָה מְבֹרָךְ מֵעַתָּה וְעַד עוֹלָם. מִמִּזְרַח שֶׁמֶשׁ עַד מְבוֹאוֹ מְהֻלָּל שֵׁם יְהוָה. רָם עַל כָּל גּוֹיִם יְהוָה עַל הַשָּׁמַיִם כְּבוֹדוֹ. מִי כַּיהוָה אֱלֹהֵינוּ הַמַּגְבִּיהִי לָשָׁבֶת. הַמַּשְׁפִּילִי לִרְאוֹת בַּשָּׁמַיִם וּבָאָרֶץ. מְקִימִי מֵעָפָר דָּל מֵאַשְׁפֹּת יָרִים אֶבְיוֹן. לְהוֹשִׁיבִי עִם נְדִיבִים עִם נְדִיבֵי עַמּוֹ. מוֹשִׁיבִי עֲקֶרֶת הַבַּיִת אֵם הַבָּנִים שְׂמֵחָה הַלְלוּיָהּ.

Halleluya heleylu avdey Adonay haleylu et shem Adonai. Yehi shem Adonai mevorach m'ata v'ad olam. Mi-mizrach shemesh ad mevo'o mehulal shem Adonay. Ram al kol goyim Adonay al ha-shamayim kevodo. Mi k'Adonay eloheynu ha'magbihi lashavet. Ha-mashpili lirot ba-shamayim u'va-aretz. Mekimi m'afar dal m'ashpot yarim evyon. L'hoshivi im nedivim im nedivey amo. Moshivi akeret ha-bayit em ha-banim semeycha halleluyah.

Praise the Lord, servants of G-d, praise G-d's name. May G-d's name be blessed from now and forever. From the sun in the East until its approach G-d's name is exalted. G-d is greater than any nation and His honor dwells in the sky. Who is like the Lord our G-d, who resides in the heavens. Who deigns to look down upon heavens and earth. He raises the poor from the dust and the needy from the ashes. He puts me with the most generous of His people. He brings joy to the housewife, mother of children. Halleluyah.

בְּצֵאת יִשְׂרָאֵל מִמִּצְרָיִם בֵּית יַעֲקֹב מֵעַם לֹעֵז. הָיְתָה יְהוּדָה לְקָדְשׁוֹ יִשְׂרָאֵל מַמְשְׁלוֹתָיו. הַיָּם רָאָה וַיָּנֹס הַיַּרְדֵּן יִסֹּב לְאָחוֹר. הֶהָרִים רָקְדוּ כְאֵילִים גְּבָעוֹת כִּבְנֵי צֹאן. מַה לְּךָ הַיָּם כִּי תָנוּס הַיַּרְדֵּן תִּסֹּב לְאָחוֹר. הֶהָרִים תִּרְקְדוּ כְאֵילִים גְּבָעוֹת כִּבְנֵי צֹאן. מִלִּפְנֵי אָדוֹן חוּלִי אָרֶץ מִלִּפְנֵי אֱלוֹהַּ יַעֲקֹב. הַהֹפְכִי הַצּוּר אֲגַם מָיִם חַלָּמִישׁ לְמַעְיְנוֹ מָיִם.

B'tseyt Yisrael m'mitzrayim beyt ya'akov me'am lo'ez. Hayta Yehuda l'kodsho Yisrael mamshelotav. Ha-yam ra'ah va-yanos ha-yarden yisov l'achor. He-harim rakdu k'eylim geva'ot kivney tson. Ma lecha ha-yam ki tanus ha-yarden tisov l'achor. He-harim tirkedu k'eylim geva'oy kivney tson. Mi-lifney Adonai chuli aretz mi-lifney eloha ya'akov. Ha-hofchi ha-tsur agam mayim chalamish l-mayno mayim.

When the Israelites left Egypt, when the house of Jacob left that foreign land, thus Jews hold Him sacred and Israel follow Him. The sea beheld and withdrew, the Jordan turned back. The mountains danced like rams, the hills like sheep and goats. Why do you withdraw, sea? Why do you turn back, Jordan? Mountains, dance like rams and hills, dance like sheep and goats. Before the Master of all, before the god of Jacob, the earth bows. You who can turn stone into water, flint into a spring.

בָּרוּךְ אַתָּה יְיָ אֱלֹהֵינוּ מֶלֶךְ הָעוֹלָם, אֲשֶׁר גְּאָלָנוּ וְגָאַל אֶת אֲבוֹתֵינוּ מִמִּצְרַיִם, וְהִגִּיעָנוּ לַלַּיְלָה הַזֶּה לֶאֱכָל בּוֹ מַצָּה וּמָרוֹר. כֵּן יְיָ אֱלֹהֵינוּ וֵאלֹהֵי אֲבוֹתֵינוּ יַגִּיעֵנוּ לְמוֹעֲדִים וְלִרְגָלִים אֲחֵרִים הַבָּאִים לִקְרָאתֵנוּ לְשָׁלוֹם, שְׂמֵחִים בְּבִנְיַן עִירֶךָ וְשָׂשִׂים בַּעֲבוֹדָתֶךָ. וְנֹאכַל שָׁם מִן הַזְּבָחִים וּמִן הַפְּסָחִים אֲשֶׁר יַגִּיעַ דָּמָם עַל קִיר מִזְבַּחֲךָ לְרָצוֹן, וְנוֹדֶה לְךָ שִׁיר חָדָשׁ עַל גְּאֻלָּתֵנוּ וְעַל פְּדוּת נַפְשֵׁנוּ. בָּרוּךְ אַתָּה יְיָ גָּאַל יִשְׂרָאֵל.

Baruch ata Adonay eloheynu Melech ha-olam, asher ge'alanu v'ga'al et avoteynu mi-mitsrayim, v'hegiyanu la'lalyla hazeh l'echol bo matzah u'maror. Ken Adonay eloheynu v'elohey avoteynu y'gi'eynu l'mo'adim u'l'regalim acherim ha-bai'im likrateynu l'shalom, semeychim b'vinyan irecha v'sasim b'avodatecha. V'nochal sham min ha-zevachim u'min ha-pesachim asher yagi-ya damam al kir mizbacheycha l'ratzon, v'nodeh lecha shir chadash al ge'ulateynu v'al pedut nafsheynu. Baruch atah Adonay ga'al Yisrael.

Blessed are You, Lord our G-d, King of the universe, who delivered us and our forefathers from Egypt, and brought us to this night, to eat matzah and maror. Lord our G-d, G-d of our ancestors, so You shall deliver us to many forthcoming events and celebrations, and we will be joyful in the resurrection of Your city and happy in doing Your work. And there, we shall eat from the sacrifices and the offerings whose blood shall touch the walls of the altar, and thank you with a new song for our salvation and the redemption of our soul

בָּרוּךְ אַתָּה יְיָ אֱלֹהֵינוּ מֶלֶךְ הָעוֹלָם בּוֹרֵא פְּרִי הַגָּפֶן.

Baruch atah Adonai Eloheinu melech ha-olam, borei peri ha-gafen.

Blessed are You, Lord our G-d, King of the universe, creator of the fruit of the vine. Israel in Academia

   Drink the second cup of wine, reclining to the left.

Did you know?

Israel is the size of New Jersey, and driving its entire length from North to South will take you only six hours. If you were to drive its width, from East to West, you would be traveling by car for no more than 90 minutes.

Did you know?

Israel has an exceptionally high fertility rate, in part thanks to its policies regarding in-vitro fertilization. IVF is performed more times per capita than in any other country, and every woman in the country is entitled to her first two rounds of IVF completely free.

Israel in Academia

Academic Publications

Israeli academic institutes have the highest number of scientific papers published per capita of any other country in the world. Israel pioneers the world of scientific discovery, making particular waves in fields such as agricultural tech, biotechnology, information technology and cyber security, water solutions, neuroscience, and genetics.

Nobel Prizes

Israel has a distinguished record of Nobel Prize winners, particularly in the fields of Chemistry, Economics, Literature, and Peace. Israeli academics' groundbreaking work has led to scientific discoveries, significant progress in curing chronic diseases, and a better general understanding of the world we live in. Israeli Nobel laureates also include those who have made significant contributions to peace and literature, showcasing the broad impact of Israeli intellect and innovation.

The Weizmann Institute

The Weizmann Institute of Science is one of the world's leading multidisciplinary research institutions. With significant contributions to the natural and exact sciences, the institute is renowned for its cutting-edge research and innovation, often translating scientific discoveries into practical applications that benefit society as a whole. The Weizmann Institute also plays a vital role in education, training the next generation of scientists through its graduate programs and international collaborations.

Israel in Archaeology

Israel's unique geographical location at the crossroads of several ancient civilizations has made it a focal point for archaeological research. Excavations in sites such as Jerusalem, Masada, Megiddo, and Qumran have unearthed artifacts and structures that shed light on the historical and cultural contexts of biblical narratives and other ancient texts. Through these endeavors, archaeology in Israel continues to reveal the complex layers of human history that have shaped the region and its cultural heritage.

Did you know?

Every single book printed in Israel must have one copy sent to Israel's National Library. The library holds a huge archive with both print and digital copies of every Israeli book ever published.

Rachtzah

רַחְצָה

Washing Hands
(this time, with a blessing)

☞ Wash your hands again, pouring water from a cup onto each hand three times.

📜 This time, recite the blessing:

בָּרוּךְ אַתָּה יְיָ אֱלֹהֵינוּ מֶלֶךְ הָעוֹלָם, אֲשֶׁר קִדְּשָׁנוּ בְּמִצְוֹתָיו וְצִוָּנוּ עַל נְטִילַת יָדָיִם.

Baruch atah Adonai Eloheinu melech ha-olam, asher kideshanu b'mitzvotav v'tzivanu al netilat yadayim.

Blessed are You, Lord our G-d, King of the universe, who has sanctified us with His commandments and commanded us to wash our hands.

Motzi-Matzah

מוֹצִיא מַצָּה

Blessing on the Matzah

☞ Pick up the three matzahs – the two whole ones with the broken half in between them – and raise them in the air.

📜 Recite the blessing:

בָּרוּךְ אַתָּה יְיָ אֱלֹהֵינוּ מֶלֶךְ הָעוֹלָם הַמּוֹצִיא לֶחֶם מִן הָאָרֶץ.

Baruch atah Adonai Eloheinu melech ha-olam, ha-motzi lech-em min ha-aretz.

Blessed are You, Lord our G-d, King of the universe, who produces bread from the earth.

☞ Now, remove the bottom matzah from the pile and return it to its place. Holding only the top and middle matzahs, recite the following blessing:

בָּרוּךְ אַתָּה יְיָ אֱלֹהֵינוּ מֶלֶךְ הָעוֹלָם, אֲשֶׁר קִדְּשָׁנוּ בְּמִצְוֹתָיו וְצִוָּנוּ עַל אֲכִילַת מַצָּה.

Baruch atah Adonai Eloheinu melech ha-olam, asher kide-shanu b'mitzvotav v'tzivanu al achilat matzah.

Blessed are You, Lord our G-d, King of the universe, who has sanctified us with His commandments and commanded us to eat matzah.

☞ Break off pieces of the top and middle matzahs and distribute them around the table. The matzah should be eaten while reclining to the left.

Israel in Philanthropy

Good Deeds Day

Israeli Good Deeds Day, initiated by businesswoman and philanthropist Shari Arison, is an annual event dedicated to encouraging individuals and organizations to engage in acts of kindness and community service. Activities range from environmental cleanups and blood donations to helping the elderly and supporting underprivileged families. Good Deeds Day has inspired a global movement, proving that small acts of kindness can have a significant impact on society.

Medical Clowns

Israel is a pioneer in the field of medical clowns, a practice that uses humor and play to support the emotional well-being of patients, particularly children. The concept of medical clowning in Israel was significantly advanced by organizations like Clown Me In and the Israel Center for Medical Clowning, which have established protocols for integrating clowns into healthcare settings to alleviate stress and pain.

The Israeli Cancer Research Fund

The ICRF is a leading non-profit organization dedicated to advancing cancer research. The organization's contributions have led to significant breakthroughs, including advancements in targeted therapies and personalized medicine. ICRF funds not only basic research but also clinical trials and translational research, bridging the gap between laboratory discoveries and patient care.

The Ruderman Family Foundation

Founded by Jay and Shira Ruderman, the Ruderman Family Foundation supports initiatives related to disability inclusion and Jewish community development. With a focus on promoting the inclusion of people with disabilities in all aspects of society, the foundation funds projects in Israel and the U.S. Its work includes advocacy, education, and creating opportunities for people with disabilities to lead fulfilling lives.

Did you know?

Tel Aviv has been crowned the world's most gay-friendly city, and celebrates Pride Month every year with an extravagant parade that draws participants from across the globe. It is also considered one of the most vegan-friendly cities to visit.

Maror

מָרוֹר

Bitter Herb

☞ Take a piece of maror (horseradish, lettuce, or another bitter herb) and dip it in the charoset.

📜 Recite the blessing before eating:

בָּרוּךְ אַתָּה יְיָ אֱלֹהֵינוּ מֶלֶךְ הָעוֹלָם, אֲשֶׁר קִדְּשָׁנוּ בְּמִצְוֹתָיו וְצִוָּנוּ עַל אֲכִילַת מָרוֹר.

Baruch atah Adonai Eloheinu melech ha-olam, asher kide-shanu b'mitzvotav v'tzivanu al achilat maror.

Blessed are You, Lord our G-d, King of the universe, who has sanctified us with His commandments and commanded us to eat a bitter herb.

☞ Do not lean while eating the Maror.

Korech

כּוֹרֵךְ

Maror Wrapped in Matzah

☞ Take two pieces of matzah, put some maror between them, and dip everything in the charoset. You may also spread the charoset on the matzah, add the maror and eat it like a sandwich.

📜 Recite before eating:

זֵכֶר לְמִקְדָּשׁ כְּהִלֵּל. כֵּן עָשָׂה הִלֵּל בִּזְמַן שֶׁבֵּית הַמִּקְדָּשׁ הָיָה קַיָּם: הָיָה כּוֹרֵךְ פסח מַצָּה וּמָרוֹר וְאוֹכֵל בְּיַחַד, לְקַיֵּם מַה שֶּׁנֶּאֱמַר: עַל מַצּוֹת וּמְרֹרִים יֹאכְלֻהוּ.

Zecher l'mikdash k'hillel. Ken asah hillel bizman she-beyt ha-mikdash hayah kayam. Hayah korech pesach matzah umaror v'ochel beyachad, lekayem mah she-ne'emar: al matzot umerowrim yocheluhu.

In memory of the custom of Hillel in the days of the Temple. So Hillel would do while there was a temple: he would wrap the matzah with the maror and eat them together, to observe what is commanded: You shall eat it (the Passover sacrifice) on matzah and maror.

☞ Recline to the left and eat the maror sandwich.

Shulchan-Orech
שֻׁלְחָן עוֹרֵךְ
The Festive Meal

☞ Now is the time to sit back, relax, and enjoy a delicious festive meal.

☞ At this point, it is customary to eat the hard-boiled egg from the Seder plate, dipped in salt water.

Israel in Education

The Technion

The Technion is one of Israel's premier institutions for higher education and research, globally recognized for its contributions to science and engineering. The Technion's innovation and research initiatives have led to numerous technological advancements and startup companies, positioning it as a leading hub for technological education and development

STEM Education

Israel places a strong emphasis on STEM (Science, Technology, Engineering, and Mathematics) education for both boys and girls, starting from an early age. Programs and initiatives such as the "Israel Science Foundation" and various science and technology centers aim to foster interest and excellence in these fields. Schools and educational institutions frequently organize science fairs, competitions, and specialized courses to engage students in STEM subjects.

Innovative Teaching Methods

Israeli educational institutions are known to frequently collaborate with international universities and research centers, contributing to global educational initiatives and research projects. Programs such as joint degrees, research partnerships, and exchange programs facilitate cross-cultural learning and broaden educational horizons in Israel and beyond its small borders.

Inclusive Education

Programs and resources are in place in Israel to support students with special needs and those from less privileged backgrounds, providing them with the tools and support necessary to succeed academically. Teaching institutions employ individualized education plans, integration programs, collaborative initiatives, and special education resources to allow students with diverse needs access to quality education and opportunities to succeed.

Did you know?

The most common street name in Israel is "Ha-Zayit" – olive-tree street. Olives are grown and exported en masse from Israel all over the world, thanks to its Mediterranean climate.

Tzafun
צָפוּן
The Afikoman

☞ Now that you've finished the meal, it's time to reveal the Afikoman.

☞ If you hid it earlier in the evening, now is the time for whoever found it during the Seder to reveal it.

☞ The Afikoman is the last thing we eat during the Seder night. Break off pieces of the Afikoman matzah and distribute them around the table. Eat the matzah while reclining to your left.

Barech

בָּרֵךְ

Blessing After the Meal

Pour the third cup of wine.

 Recite the blessing on the wine:

בָּרוּךְ אַתָּה יְיָ אֱלֹהֵינוּ מֶלֶךְ הָעוֹלָם בּוֹרֵא פְּרִי הַגָּפֶן.

Baruch atah Adonai Eloheinu melech ha-olam, borei peri ha-gafen.

Blessed are You, Lord our G-d, King of the universe, creator of the fruit of the vine.

 Drink the third cup of wine, while reclining to the left.

 Pour the fourth cup of wine.

 It is customary to pour an extra cup of wine for Elijah the Prophet, who is said to visit on Seder night. Open the front door to invite him in.

Recite the following:

שְׁפֹךְ חֲמָתְךָ אֶל הַגּוֹיִם אֲשֶׁר לֹא יְדָעוּךָ וְעַל מַמְלָכוֹת אֲשֶׁר בְּשִׁמְךָ לֹא קָרָאוּ. כִּי אָכַל אֶת יַעֲקֹב וְאֶת נָוֵהוּ הֵשַׁמּוּ. שְׁפֹךְ עֲלֵיהֶם זַעְמֶךָ וַחֲרוֹן אַפְּךָ יַשִּׂיגֵם. תִּרְדֹּף בְּאַף וְתַשְׁמִידֵם מִתַּחַת שְׁמֵי יְיָ.

Shefoch chamatcha el ha-goyim asher lo yeda'ucha v'al mamlachot asher b'shimcha lo kar'u. Ki achal et ya'akov v'et navehu heyshamu. Shefoch aleyhem za'amcha v'charon apcha yasigem. Tirdof b'af v'tashmidem mitachat shmey Adonai.

Unleash Your wrath upon the nations who do not acknowledge You and upon the kingdoms who do not call Your Name. For they have devoured Jacob and destroyed his land. Unleash Your fury upon them and let Your anger seize them. Pursue them with rage and destroy them beneath G-d's heavens.

Some sing Eliyahu Ha'navi, which can be found in the "Songs" section on page 96.

You may now close the front door.

Did you know?

Israelis are the biggest consumers of fruits and vegetables per capita. In fact, it is common to eat vegetables for every single meal of the day, including breakfast!

Did you know?

Thanks in part to Bamba, a popular peanut-based, infant-friendly Israeli snack, babies in Israel are 10 times less likely to develop a peanut allergy than babies in other countries.

Hallel

הַלֵּל

Praise to G-d

הִנְנִי מוּכָן וּמְזֻמָּן לְקַיֵּם מִצְוַת כּוֹס רְבִיעִי שֶׁהוּא כְּנֶגֶד בְּשׂוֹרַת הַיְשׁוּעָה, שֶׁאָמַר הַקָּדוֹשׁ בָּרוּךְ הוּא לְיִשְׂרָאֵל "וְלָקַחְתִּי אֶתְכֶם לִי לְעָם וְהָיִיתִי לָכֶם לֵאלֹהִים".

Hineyni muchan u'mezuman l'kayem mitzvat kos revi'i she-hu k'negged besorat ha-yeshu'a, she-amar ha-Kadosh Baruch Hu l'Yisrael, "v'lakachti etchem li l'am v'hayiti lachem l'elohim."

I am ready and willing to observe the commandment of the fourth cup, which signifies the tidings of salvation, as G-d said to the people of Israel: "and I will take you in as my people and I shall be your god."

 Now, make a blessing on the fourth cup of wine:

בָּרוּךְ אַתָּה יְיָ אֱלֹהֵינוּ מֶלֶךְ הָעוֹלָם בּוֹרֵא פְּרִי הַגָּפֶן.

Baruch atah Adonai Eloheinu melech ha-olam, borei peri ha-gafen.

Blessed are You, Lord our G-d, King of the universe, creator of the fruit of the vine.

 Drink the fourth and final cup of wine while reclining to the left.

 Recite the final blessing after drinking wine:

בָּרוּךְ אַתָּה יְיָ אֱלֹהֵינוּ מֶלֶךְ הָעוֹלָם, עַל הַגֶּפֶן וְעַל פְּרִי הַגֶּפֶן, עַל תְּנוּבַת הַשָּׂדֶה וְעַל אֶרֶץ חֶמְדָּה טוֹבָה וּרְחָבָה שֶׁרָצִיתָ וְהִנְחַלְתָּ לַאֲבוֹתֵינוּ לֶאֱכֹל מִפִּרְיָהּ וְלִשְׂבֹּעַ מִטּוּבָהּ.

Baruch atah Adonai Eloheinu melech ha-olam, al ha-gefen v'al peri ha-gefen, al tnuvat ha-sadeh v'al eretz chemda tova u'rechava she-ratsita v'hinchalta l'avoteynu le'echol m'pirya v'lisbo'a mituva.

Blessed are You, Lord our G-d, King of the universe, for the vines and the fruit of the vines, for the produce of the field, and for the good, beautiful and vast country which You chose to give to our ancestors so that we may eat from its fruit and be satiated by its goodness.

רַחֵם נָא יְיָ אֱלֹהֵינוּ עַל יִשְׂרָאֵל עַמֶּךָ וְעַל יְרוּשָׁלַיִם עִירֶךָ וְעַל צִיּוֹן מִשְׁכַּן כְּבוֹדֶךָ וְעַל מִזְבְּחֶךָ וְעַל הֵיכָלֶךָ וּבְנֵה יְרוּשָׁלַיִם עִיר הַקֹּדֶשׁ בִּמְהֵרָה בְיָמֵינוּ וְהַעֲלֵנוּ לְתוֹכָהּ וְשַׂמְּחֵנוּ בְּבִנְיָנָהּ וְנֹאכַל מִפִּרְיָהּ וְנִשְׂבַּע מִטּוּבָהּ וּנְבָרֶכְךָ עָלֶיהָ בִּקְדֻשָּׁה וּבְטָהֳרָה.

Rachem na Adonai Eloheinu al Yisrael amcha v'al yerushalayim irecha v'al tsion mishkan kevodecha v'al mizbachecha v'al heichalecha u'vney yerushalayim ir ha-kodesh bimhera b'yameynu v'ha'aleynu l'tochah v'samchenu b'vinyanah v'nochal m'pirya v'nisba mituva u'nevarechecha aleyha b'kdusha uv'tahara.

Please have mercy, Lord our G-d, on Israel Your people, on Jerusalem Your city, on Zion, Your place of rest, on Your altar and Your hall. Rebuild the holy city of Jerusalem in our time and let us ascend to it and be joyous in its grandeur. Then we shall eat from its fruit and be satiated by its goodness and bless You for it with sanctity and purity.

בְּשַׁבָּת: וּרְצֵה וְהַחֲלִיצֵנוּ בְּיוֹם הַשַּׁבָּת הַזֶּה) וְשַׂמְּחֵנוּ בְּיוֹם חַג הַמַּצּוֹת הַזֶּה, כִּי אַתָּה יְיָ טוֹב וּמֵטִיב לַכֹּל וְנוֹדֶה לְּךָ עַל הָאָרֶץ וְעַל פְּרִי הַגָּפֶן.

(on Shabbat: u'retsey v'hachalitseynu b'yom ha-shabbat hazeh) v'samcheynu b'yom chag ha-matzot hazeh, ki atah Adonai tov u'meytiv lakol v'nodeh lecha al ha'aretz v'al peri ha-gafen.

(On Shabbat: Give us strength on this Sabbath day and) let us be happy on this festival of Matzah, because You are good and benevolent to all and we will thank You for the land and for the fruit of the vine.

בָּרוּךְ אַתָּה יְיָ עַל הָאָרֶץ וְעַל פְּרִי הַגָּפֶן.

Baruch ata Adonai, al ha'aretz v'al peri ha-gafen.

Blessed are You, G-d, for the land and for the fruit of the vine.

Nirtzah

נִרְצָה

Conclusion of the Seder

☞ At the conclusion of the Seder, we celebrate having been able to come together for the festivities and look forward to a prosperous and happy year. Everyone sings together:

לְשָׁנָה הַבָּאָה בִּירוּשָׁלָיִם.   L'shana haba'ah b'Yerushalayim

Next year in Jerusalem!

Songs

Chad Gadya – One Little Goat

חַד גַּדְיָא, חַד גַּדְיָא, דְּזַבִּין אַבָּא בִּתְרֵי זוּזֵי, חַד גַּדְיָא, חַד גַּדְיָא.

וְאָתָא שׁוּנְרָא וְאָכְלָה לְגַדְיָא, דְּזַבִּין אַבָּא בִּתְרֵי זוּזֵי, חַד גַּדְיָא, חַד גַּדְיָא.

וְאָתָא כַלְבָּא וְנָשַׁךְ לְשׁוּנְרָא, דְּאָכְלָה לְגַדְיָא, דְּזַבִּין אַבָּא בִּתְרֵי זוּזֵי, חַד גַּדְיָא, חַד גַּדְיָא.

וְאָתָא חוּטְרָא וְהִכָּה לְכַלְבָּא, דְּנָשַׁךְ לְשׁוּנְרָא, דְּאָכְלָה לְגַדְיָא, דְּזַבִּין אַבָּא בִּתְרֵי זוּזֵי, חַד גַּדְיָא, חַד גַּדְיָא.

וְאָתָא נוּרָא וְשָׂרַף לְחוּטְרָא, דְּהִכָּה לְכַלְבָּא, דְּנָשַׁךְ לְשׁוּנְרָא, דְּאָכְלָה לְגַדְיָא, דְּזַבִּין אַבָּא בִּתְרֵי זוּזֵי, חַד גַּדְיָא, חַד גַּדְיָא.

וְאָתָא מַיָּא וְכָבָה לְנוּרָא, דְּשָׂרַף לְחוּטְרָא, דְּהִכָּה לְכַלְבָּא, דְּנָשַׁךְ לְשׁוּנְרָא, דְּאָכְלָה לְגַדְיָא, דְּזַבִּין אַבָּא בִּתְרֵי זוּזֵי, חַד גַּדְיָא, חַד גַּדְיָא.

Chad gadya, chad gadya, d'zabin aba b'trei zuzei, chad gadya, chad gadya.

V'ata shunra v'achla l'gadya, d'zabin aba b'trei zuzei, chad gadya, chad gadya.

V'ata chalba v'nashach l'shunra, d'achla l'gadya, d'zabin aba b'trei zuzei, chad gadya, chad gadya.

V'ata chutra v'hica l'calba, d'nashach l'shunra, d'achla l'gadya, d'zabin aba b'trei zuzei, chad gadya, chad gadya.

V'ata nura v'saraf l'chutra, d'hica l'calba, d'nashach l'shunra, d'achla l'gadya, d'zabin aba b'trei zuzei, chad gadya, chad gadya.

V'ata maya v'chaba l'nura, d'saraf l'chutra, d'hica l'calba, d'nashach l'shunra, d'achla l'gadya, d'zabin aba b'trei zuzei, chad gadya, chad gadya.

וְאָתָא תוֹרָא וְשָׁתָה לְמַיָּא, דְּכָבָה לְנוּרָא, דְּשָׂרַף לְחוּטְרָא, דְּהִכָּה לְכַלְבָּא, דְּנָשַׁךְ לְשׁוּנְרָא, דְּאָכְלָה לְגַדְיָא, דְּזַבִּין אַבָּא בִּתְרֵי זוּזֵי, חַד גַּדְיָא, חַד גַּדְיָא.

V'ata tora v'shata l'maya, d'chaba l'nura, d'saraf l'chutra, d'hica l'calba, d'nashach l'shunra, d'achla l'gadya, d'zabin aba b'trei zuzei, chad gadya, chad gadya.

וְאָתָא הַשּׁוֹחֵט וְשָׁחַט לְתוֹרָא, דְּשָׁתָה לְמַיָּא, דְּכָבָה לְנוּרָא, דְּשָׂרַף לְחוּטְרָא, דְּהִכָּה לְכַלְבָּא, דְּנָשַׁךְ לְשׁוּנְרָא, דְּאָכְלָה לְגַדְיָא, דְּזַבִּין אַבָּא בִּתְרֵי זוּזֵי, חַד גַּדְיָא, חַד גַּדְיָא.

V'ata hashochet v'shachat l'tora, d'shata l'maya, d'chaba l'nura, d'saraf l'chutra, d'hica l'calba, d'nashach l'shunra, d'achla l'gadya, d'zabin aba b'trei zuzei, chad gadya, chad gadya.

וְאָתָא מַלְאַךְ הַמָּוֶת וְשָׁחַט לְשׁוֹחֵט, דְּשָׁחַט לְתוֹרָא, דְּשָׁתָה לְמַיָּא, דְּכָבָה לְנוּרָא, דְּשָׂרַף לְחוּטְרָא, דְּהִכָּה לְכַלְבָּא, דְּנָשַׁךְ לְשׁוּנְרָא, דְּאָכְלָה לְגַדְיָא, דְּזַבִּין אַבָּא בִּתְרֵי זוּזֵי, חַד גַּדְיָא, חַד גַּדְיָא.

V'ata malach hamavet v'shachat l'shochet, d'shachat l'tora, d'shata l'maya, d'chaba l'nura, d'saraf l'chutra, d'hica l'calba, d'nashach l'shunra, d'achla l'gadya, d'zabin aba b'trei zuzei, chad gadya, chad gadya.

וְאָתָא הַקָּדוֹשׁ בָּרוּךְ הוּא וְשָׁחַט לְמַלְאַךְ הַמָּוֶת, דְּשָׁחַט לְשׁוֹחֵט, דְּשָׁחַט לְתוֹרָא, דְּשָׁתָה לְמַיָּא, דְּכָבָה לְנוּרָא, דְּשָׂרַף לְחוּטְרָא, דְּהִכָּה לְכַלְבָּא, דְּנָשַׁךְ לְשׁוּנְרָא, דְּאָכְלָה לְגַדְיָא דְּזַבִּין אַבָּא בִּתְרֵי זוּזֵי, חַד גַּדְיָא, חַד גַּדְיָא.

V'ata ha-Kadosh Baruch Hu, v'ishachat l'malach hamavet, d'shachat l'shochet, d'shachat l'tora, d'shata l'maya, d'chaba l'nura, d'saraf l'chutra, d'hica l'calba, d'nashach l'shunra, d'achla l'gadya, d'zabin aba b'trei zuzei, chad gadya, chad gadya.

One little goat, one little goat that father bought for two zuzim. One little goat, one little goat.

Along came a cat and ate the goat that father bought for two zuzim. One little goat, one little goat.

Along came a dog and bit the cat that ate the goat that father bought for two zuzim. One little goat, one little goat.

Along came a stick and hit the dog that bit the cat that ate the goat that father bought for two zuzim. One little goat, one little goat.

Along came a fire and burned the stick that hit the dog that bit the cat that ate the goat that father bought for two zuzim. One little goat, one little goat.

Along came some water and put out the fire that burned the stick that hit the dog that bit the cat that ate the goat that father bought for two zuzim. One little goat, one little goat.

Along came an ox and drank the water that put out the fire that burned the stick that hit the dog that bit the cat that ate the goat that father bought for two zuzim. One little goat, one little goat.

Along came a butcher and slaughtered the ox that drank the water that put out the fire that burned the stick that hit the dog that bit the cat that ate the goat that father bought for two zuzim. One little goat, one little goat.

Along came the angel of death and slaughtered the butcher who slaughtered the ox that drank the water that put out the fire that burned the stick that hit the dog that bit the cat that ate the goat that father bought for two zuzim. One little goat, one little goat.

Then along came the Holy One, Blessed be He, and slaughtered the angel of death who slaughtered the butcher who slaughtered the ox that drank the water that put out the fire that burned the stick that hit the dog that bit the cat that ate the goat that father bought for two zuzim. One little goat, one little goat.

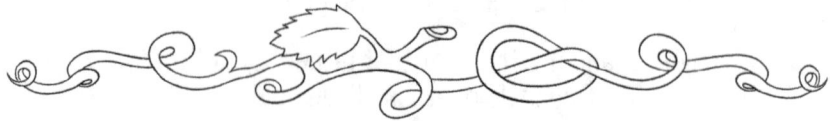

Echad Mi Yodeya – Who Knows One?

אֶחָד מִי יוֹדֵעַ? אֶחָד אֲנִי יוֹדֵעַ. אֶחָד אֱלֹהֵינוּ שֶׁבַּשָּׁמַיִם וּבָאָרֶץ.

שְׁנַיִם מִי יוֹדֵעַ? שְׁנַיִם אֲנִי יוֹדֵעַ. שְׁנֵי לוּחוֹת הַבְּרִית, אֶחָד אֱלֹהֵינוּ שֶׁבַּשָּׁמַיִם וּבָאָרֶץ.

שְׁלֹשָׁה מִי יוֹדֵעַ? שְׁלֹשָׁה אֲנִי יוֹדֵעַ. שְׁלֹשָׁה אָבוֹת, שְׁנֵי לוּחוֹת הַבְּרִית, אֶחָד אֱלֹהֵינוּ שֶׁבַּשָּׁמַיִם וּבָאָרֶץ.

אַרְבַּע מִי יוֹדֵעַ? אַרְבַּע אֲנִי יוֹדֵעַ. אַרְבַּע אִמָּהוֹת, שְׁלֹשָׁה אָבוֹת, שְׁנֵי לוּחוֹת הַבְּרִית, אֶחָד אֱלֹהֵינוּ שֶׁבַּשָּׁמַיִם וּבָאָרֶץ.

חֲמִשָּׁה מִי יוֹדֵעַ? חֲמִשָּׁה אֲנִי יוֹדֵעַ. חֲמִשָּׁה חֻמְשֵׁי תּוֹרָה, אַרְבַּע אִמָּהוֹת, שְׁלֹשָׁה אָבוֹת, שְׁנֵי לוּחוֹת הַבְּרִית, אֶחָד אֱלֹהֵינוּ שֶׁבַּשָּׁמַיִם וּבָאָרֶץ.

שִׁשָּׁה מִי יוֹדֵעַ? שִׁשָּׁה אֲנִי יוֹדֵעַ. שִׁשָּׁה סִדְרֵי מִשְׁנָה, חֲמִשָּׁה חֻמְשֵׁי תּוֹרָה, אַרְבַּע אִמָּהוֹת, שְׁלֹשָׁה אָבוֹת, שְׁנֵי לוּחוֹת הַבְּרִית, אֶחָד אֱלֹהֵינוּ שֶׁבַּשָּׁמַיִם וּבָאָרֶץ.

Echad mi yodea? Echad ani yodea. Echad Eloheinu she-bashamayim u'va'aretz.

Shnayim mi yodea? Shnayim ani yodea. Shnei luchot ha-brit, echad Eloheinu she-bashamayim u'va'aretz.

Shloshah mi yodea? Shloshah ani yodea. Shloshah avot, shnei luchot ha-brit, echad Eloheinu she-bashamayim u'va'aretz.

Arbah mi yodea? Arbah ani yodea. Arbah imahot, shloshah avot, shnei luchot ha-brit, echad Eloheinu she-bashamayim u'va'aretz.

Chamishah mi yodea? Chamishah ani yodea. Chamishah chumshei Torah, arbah imahot, shloshah avot, shnei luchot ha-brit, echad Eloheinu she-bashamayim u'va'aretz.

Shishah mi yodea? Shishah ani yodea. Shishah sidrei mishnah, chamishah chumshei Torah, arbah imahot, shloshah avot, shnei luchot ha-brit, echad Eloheinu she-bashamayim u'va'aretz.

שִׁבְעָה מִי יוֹדֵעַ? שִׁבְעָה אֲנִי יוֹדֵעַ. שִׁבְעָה יְמֵי שַׁבַּתָּא, שִׁשָּׁה סִדְרֵי מִשְׁנָה, חֲמִשָּׁה חֻמְשֵׁי תוֹרָה, אַרְבַּע אִמָּהוֹת, שְׁלֹשָׁה אָבוֹת, שְׁנֵי לוּחוֹת הַבְּרִית, אֶחָד אֱלֹהֵינוּ שֶׁבַּשָּׁמַיִם וּבָאָרֶץ.

Shivah mi yodea? Shivah ani yodea. Shivah y'mei shabtah, shishah sidrei mishnah, chamishah chumshei Torah, arbah imahot, shloshah avot, shnei luchot ha-brit, echad Eloheinu she-bashamayim u'va'aretz.

שְׁמוֹנָה מִי יוֹדֵעַ? שְׁמוֹנָה אֲנִי יוֹדֵעַ. שְׁמוֹנָה יְמֵי מִילָה, שִׁבְעָה יְמֵי שַׁבַּתָּא, שִׁשָּׁה סִדְרֵי מִשְׁנָה, חֲמִשָּׁה חֻמְשֵׁי תוֹרָה, אַרְבַּע אִמָּהוֹת, שְׁלֹשָׁה אָבוֹת, שְׁנֵי לוּחוֹת הַבְּרִית, אֶחָד אֱלֹהֵינוּ שֶׁבַּשָּׁמַיִם וּבָאָרֶץ.

Shmonah mi yodea? Shmonah ani yodea. Shmonah y'mei milah, shivah y'mei shabtah, shishah sidrei mishnah, chamishah chumshei Torah, arbah imahot, shloshah avot, shnei luchot ha-brit, echad Eloheinu she-bashamayim u'va'aretz.

תִּשְׁעָה מִי יוֹדֵעַ? תִּשְׁעָה אֲנִי יוֹדֵעַ. תִּשְׁעָה יַרְחֵי לֵדָה, שְׁמוֹנָה יְמֵי מִילָה, שִׁבְעָה יְמֵי שַׁבַּתָּא, שִׁשָּׁה סִדְרֵי מִשְׁנָה, חֲמִשָּׁה חֻמְשֵׁי תוֹרָה, אַרְבַּע אִמָּהוֹת, שְׁלֹשָׁה אָבוֹת, שְׁנֵי לוּחוֹת הַבְּרִית, אֶחָד אֱלֹהֵינוּ שֶׁבַּשָּׁמַיִם וּבָאָרֶץ.

Tishah mi yodea? Tishah ani yodea. Tishah yarchei leidah, shmonah y'mei milah, shivah y'mei shabtah, shishah sidrei mishnah, chamishah chumshei Torah, arbah imahot, shloshah avot, shnei luchot ha-brit, echad Eloheinu she-bashamayim u'va'aretz.

עֲשָׂרָה מִי יוֹדֵעַ? עֲשָׂרָה אֲנִי יוֹדֵעַ. עֲשָׂרָה דִּבְּרַיָּא, תִּשְׁעָה יַרְחֵי לֵדָה, שְׁמוֹנָה יְמֵי מִילָה, שִׁבְעָה יְמֵי שַׁבַּתָּא, שִׁשָּׁה סִדְרֵי מִשְׁנָה, חֲמִשָּׁה חֻמְשֵׁי תוֹרָה, אַרְבַּע אִמָּהוֹת, שְׁלֹשָׁה אָבוֹת, שְׁנֵי לוּחוֹת הַבְּרִית, אֶחָד אֱלֹהֵינוּ שֶׁבַּשָּׁמַיִם וּבָאָרֶץ.

Asarah mi yodea? Asarah ani yodea. Asarah dibrayah, tishah yarchei leidah, shmonah y'mei milah, shivah y'mei shabtah, shishah sidrei mishnah, chamishah chumshei Torah, arbah imahot, shloshah avot, shnei luchot ha-brit, echad Eloheinu she-bashamayim u'va'aretz.

Songs

אַחַד עָשָׂר מִי יוֹדֵעַ? אַחַד עָשָׂר אֲנִי יוֹדֵעַ. אַחַד עָשָׂר כּוֹכְבַיָּא, עֲשָׂרָה דִבְּרַיָּא, תִּשְׁעָה יַרְחֵי לֵדָה, שְׁמוֹנָה יְמֵי מִילָה, שִׁבְעָה יְמֵי שַׁבְּתָא, שִׁשָּׁה סִדְרֵי מִשְׁנָה, חֲמִשָּׁה חֻמְשֵׁי תוֹרָה, אַרְבַּע אִמָּהוֹת, שְׁלֹשָׁה אָבוֹת, שְׁנֵי לוּחוֹת הַבְּרִית, אֶחָד אֱלֹהֵינוּ שֶׁבַּשָּׁמַיִם וּבָאָרֶץ.

Achad-asar mi yodea? Achad-asar ani yodea. Achad-asar kochvayah, asarah dibrayah, tishah yarchei leidah, shmonah y'mei milah, shivah y'mei shabtah, shishah sidrei mishnah, chamishah chumshei Torah, arbah imahot, shloshah avot, shnei luchot ha-brit, echad Eloheinu she-bashamayim u'va'aretz.

שְׁנֵים עָשָׂר מִי יוֹדֵעַ? שְׁנֵים עָשָׂר אֲנִי יוֹדֵעַ. שְׁנֵים עָשָׂר שִׁבְטַיָּא, אַחַד עָשָׂר כּוֹכְבַיָּא, עֲשָׂרָה דִבְּרַיָּא, תִּשְׁעָה יַרְחֵי לֵדָה, שְׁמוֹנָה יְמֵי מִילָה, שִׁבְעָה יְמֵי שַׁבְּתָא, שִׁשָּׁה סִדְרֵי מִשְׁנָה, חֲמִשָּׁה חֻמְשֵׁי תוֹרָה, אַרְבַּע אִמָּהוֹת, שְׁלֹשָׁה אָבוֹת, שְׁנֵי לוּחוֹת הַבְּרִית, אֶחָד אֱלֹהֵינוּ שֶׁבַּשָּׁמַיִם וּבָאָרֶץ.

Shneim-asar mi yodea? Shneim-asar ani yodea. Shneim-asar shivtayah, achad-asar kochvayah, asarah dibrayah, tishah yarchei leidah, shmonah y'mei milah, shivah y'mei shabtah, shishah sidrei mishnah, chamishah chumshei Torah, arbah imahot, shloshah avot, shnei luchot ha-brit, echad Eloheinu she-bashamayim u'va'aretz.

שְׁלֹשָׁה עָשָׂר מִי יוֹדֵעַ? שְׁלֹשָׁה עָשָׂר אֲנִי יוֹדֵעַ. שְׁלֹשָׁה עָשָׂר מִדַּיָּא, שְׁנֵים עָשָׂר שִׁבְטַיָּא, אַחַד עָשָׂר כּוֹכְבַיָּא, עֲשָׂרָה דִבְּרַיָּא, תִּשְׁעָה יַרְחֵי לֵדָה, שְׁמוֹנָה יְמֵי מִילָה, שִׁבְעָה יְמֵי שַׁבְּתָא, שִׁשָּׁה סִדְרֵי מִשְׁנָה, חֲמִשָּׁה חֻמְשֵׁי תוֹרָה, אַרְבַּע אִמָּהוֹת, שְׁלֹשָׁה אָבוֹת, שְׁנֵי לוּחוֹת הַבְּרִית, אֶחָד אֱלֹהֵינוּ שֶׁבַּשָּׁמַיִם וּבָאָרֶץ.

Shloshah-asar mi yodea? Shloshah-asar ani yodea. Shloshah-asar midayah, shneim-asar shivtayah, achad-asar kochvayah, asarah dibrayah, tishah yarchei leidah, shmonah y'mei milah, shivah y'mei shabtah, shishah sidrei mishnah, chamishah chumshei Torah, arbah imahot, shloshah avot, shnei luchot ha-brit, echad Eloheinu she-bashamayim u'va'aretz.

Who knows one? I know one. One is our G-d in Heaven and Earth.

Who knows two? I know two. Two are the tablets of the covenant. One is our G-d in Heaven and Earth.

Who knows three? I know three. Three are the patriarchs. Two are the tablets of the covenant. One is our G-d in Heaven and Earth.

Who knows four? I know four. Four are the matriarchs. Three are the patriarchs. Two are the tablets of the covenant. One is our G-d in Heaven and Earth.

Who knows five? I know five. Five are the books of the Torah. Four are the matriarchs. Three are the patriarchs. Two are the tablets of the covenant. One is our G-d in Heaven and Earth.

Who knows six? I know six. Six are the orders of the Mishnah. Five are the books of the Torah. Four are the matriarchs. Three are the patriarchs. Two are the tablets of the covenant. One is our G-d in Heaven and Earth.

Who knows seven? I know seven. Seven are the days of the week. Six are the orders of the Mishnah. Five are the books of the Torah. Four are the matriarchs. Three are the patriarchs. Two are the tablets of the covenant. One is our G-d in Heaven and Earth

Who knows eight? I know eight. Eight are the days for circumcision. Seven are the days of the week. Six are the orders of the Mishnah. Five are the books of the Torah. Four are the matriarchs. Three are the patriarchs. Two are the tablets of the covenant. One is our G-d in Heaven and Earth.

Who knows nine? I know nine. Nine are the months of childbirth. Eight are the days for circumcision. Seven are the days of the week. Six are the orders of the Mishnah. Five are the books of the Torah. Four are the matriarchs. Three are the patriarchs. Two are the tablets of the covenant. One is our G-d in Heaven and Earth.

Who knows ten? I know ten. Ten are the Words from Sinai. Nine are the months of childbirth. Eight are the days for circumcision. Seven are the days of the week. Six are the orders of the Mishnah. Five are the books of the Torah. Four are the matriarchs. Three are the patriarchs. Two are the tablets of the covenant. One is our G-d in Heaven and Earth.

Who knows eleven? I know eleven. Eleven are the stars. Ten are the Words from Sinai. Nine are the months of childbirth. Eight are the days for circumcision. Seven are the days of the week. Six are the orders of the Mishnah. Five are the books of the Torah. Four are the matriarchs. Three are the patriarchs. Two are the tablets of the covenant. One is our G-d in Heaven and Earth.

Who knows twelve? I know twelve. Twelve are the tribes. Eleven are the stars. Ten are the Words from Sinai. Nine are the months of childbirth. Eight are the days for circumcision. Seven are the days of the week. Six are the orders of the Mishnah. Five are the books of the Torah. Four are the matriarchs. Three are the patriarchs. Two are the tablets of the covenant. One is our G-d in Heaven and Earth.

Who knows thirteen? I know thirteen. Thirteen are the attributes of G-d. Twelve are the tribes. Eleven are the stars. Ten are the Words from Sinai. Nine are the months of childbirth. Eight are the days for circumcision. Seven are the days of the week. Six are the orders of the Mishnah. Five are the books of the Torah. Four are the matriarchs. Three are the patriarchs. Two are the tablets of the covenant. One is our G-d in Heaven and Earth.

Eliyahu Hanavi – *The Prophet Elijah*

אֵלִיָּהוּ הַנָּבִיא, אֵלִיָּהוּ הַתִּשְׁבִּי, אֵלִיָּהוּ הַגִּלְעָדִי, בִּמְהֵרָה יָבֹא אֵלֵינוּ עִם מָשִׁיחַ בֶּן דָּוִד.

Eliyahu ha-navi, Eliyahu ha-tishbi, Eliyahu ha-giladi. Bimheirah yavo eleynu, im Mashiach ben David.

May Elijah the prophet, Elijah the Tishbite, Elijah of Gilead, quickly in our day come to us heralding redemption with the Messiah, son of David.

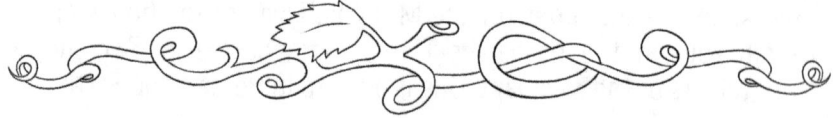

Let My People Go

"When Israel was in Egypt land, let my people go.
Oppressed so hard they could not stand, let my people go."
Go down, Moses, way down in Egypt land.
Tell old Pharaoh, let my people go!

"Thus saith the Lord" bold Moses said, "Let my people go,
If not I'll smite your firstborn dead, let my people go."
Go down, Moses, way down in Egypt land.
Tell old Pharaoh, let my people go!

"No more shall they in bondage toil, let my people go.
Let them come out with Egypt's spoils, let my people go."
Go down, Moses, way down in Egypt land.
Tell old Pharaoh, let my people go!

"When people stop this slavery, let my people go.
Soon may all the earth be free, let my people go."
Go down, Moses, way down in Egypt land.
Tell old Pharaoh, let my people go!

Appendix – Israeli Recipes

Tabbouleh Salad

Tabbouleh salad is a traditional Middle-Eastern side dish, popular in Israeli restaurants and households. Colorful and bursting with fresh vegetables and greens, it is a decorative addition to any festive table.

Ingredients (4-5 servings):

- 1.5 cups dry bulgur (or 1.5 cups quinoa, for a kosher for Passover alternative)
- 2 cups boiling water
- 0.5 cup chopped fresh parsley
- 0.45 cup chopped fresh mint leaves
- 3 large tomatoes
- 3 scallions
- 3 tbsp. olive oil
- Juice from 2 freshly squeezed lemons
- Salt & pepper to taste
- 0.5 cup pomegranate seeds (optional)

Instructions:

- Put the bulgur in a bowl with the boiling water and cover with a towel for 15 minutes until all the water has been absorbed. Separate gently with a fork.

- If substituting with quinoa for a kosher for Passover recipe, cook quinoa on low heat in 3 cups of water. Once cooked and cooled, separate gently with a fork.

- Dice the tomatoes small and chop the scallions. Add chopped parsley, mint leaves, tomatoes, and scallions to the bulgur or quinoa, once cool.

- In a separate bowl, mix olive oil, lemon juice, salt, and pepper to prepare the dressing.

- Dress and serve immediately.

- Optional – sprinkle pomegranate seeds for an extra pop of color and sweetness.

Charoset

The traditional Passover treat charoset is a mixture of apples, cinnamon, and walnuts that come together to create a sweet and symbolic dish, perfect for spreading on matzo or eating by the spoonful.

Ingredients (2 cups):

- 2 green apples
- 1 cup walnuts, chopped
- 1 tsp. ground cinnamon
- 0.25 cup sweet red wine
- 2 tbsp. honey
- 1 tbsp. freshly squeezed lemon juice
- Dates, almonds, or figs (optional)

Instructions:

- Core, peel, and dice the apples finely. Place in a mixing bowl. Add the chopped walnuts, ground cinnamon, red wine, honey, and lemon juice to the bowl and mix until well combined.

- Taste and adjust the flavors, adding honey, cinnamon, or lemon as needed.

- Chill for at least an hour before serving.

- Finely chop dates, almonds, or figs as desired and sprinkle over the charoset before serving.

Matzo-Ball Soup

Matzo-ball soup is the quintessential Jewish comfort food. Light and delicious, the stock combines flavors of chicken and vegetables and the matzo-balls add a nostalgic touch. No Passover is complete without it!

Ingredients (6-8 servings):

For the soup:

- 4 celery stalks
- Fresh parsley
- 2 carrots, halved
- 2 medium onions, halved
- 4 cloves of garlic, whole
- 4 whole chicken thighs
- 3 liters water
- Salt & pepper to taste

For the matzo balls:

- 1 cup matzo meal
- 1 tsp. baking powder
- 1 tsp. salt
- 2 tbsp. oil
- 1.5 cups boiling water
- 2 large eggs

Instructions:

- Put the celery, parsley, carrots, onions, garlic, and chicken in a large pot, cover with water, and bring to a boil. Add salt and pepper and allow to simmer for 2-3 hours, stirring and adding water as needed.

- Strain the chicken stock into another pot. You can cut the chicken and vegetables into smaller pieces and add them to the pot or leave the stock clear as it is.

- In a bowl, mix matzo meal, baking powder, salt, pepper, and oil. Add the boiling water and mix until combined. Cover and place in the fridge for 10 minutes. In a separate bowl, whisk the eggs.

- In a small pot, boil 2 liters of water with some salt. Remove the matzo ball mixture from the fridge and combine with the whisked eggs. Then, with wet hands, shape into matzo balls of your desired size. Place the balls gently in the boiling water and cook for 5-8 minutes on a low flame.

- Heat the soup before serving and add the matzo balls to warm for several minutes. Serve and enjoy!

Eggplant & Tahini Dip

This Middle-Eastern version of baba ganoush is smooth and tangy and pairs great with matzo!

Ingredients (4 servings):

- 2 whole eggplants
- 0.25 cup of raw tahini
- 2-3 cloves of garlic, crushed
- 2 tbsp. lemon juice
- Salt & pepper to taste
- Olive oil and parsley for garnishing

Instructions:

- Lightly stab all over the eggplants with a fork, then grill them whole at 420° for 40-45 minutes until they are scorched and soft.
- Let the eggplants cool before cutting them open and scraping out the light-colored meat inside. Let the filling rest in a strainer for 20-30 minutes until any spare liquids have been removed.
- Chop the eggplant finely and add it to a bowl with the tahini, garlic, lemon juice, and seasoning.
- Garnish with olive oil and chopped parsley.

Iced Limonana

Iced limonana (lemon and mint) is a classic Israeli drink to be found in any Tel Aviv café. Cold, sweet, and refreshing, it is the perfect drink for a hot Israeli summer day!

To order in Israel, ask for "limonana garus".

Ingredients (4-5 servings):

- 8 tbsp. sugar
- 0.5 cup boiling water
- 1.5 cups ice
- 1 cup fresh mint leaves
- 2 cups cold water
- Juice from 5 freshly squeezed lemons

Instructions:

- Stir the sugar into the boiling water until fully dissolved, then set aside.
- In a blender, blend the rest of the ingredients well – ice, mint, water, and lemon juice.
- Add the sugar water and mix thoroughly.
- Serve ice-cold and decorate with a slice of lemon and a sprig of mint leaves.

www.ingramcontent.com/pod-product-compliance
Lightning Source LLC
LaVergne TN
LVHW020429070526
838199LV00004B/339